$24.75

Management of
Trade Credit

Management of Trade Credit

**Thomas Guybon Hutson
and
John Butterworth**

Second Edition

Gower Press

Published in Great Britain by Gower Press Limited, Epping, Essex
First edition 1968
Second impression 1969
Second edition 1974

© T. G. Hutson and J. Butterworth, 1974

ISBN 0 7161 0234 X

Typeset in IBM Press Roman by
Preface Limited, Salisbury, Wilts
and Printed in Great Britain by
Robert MacLehose & Co. Ltd
The University Press, Glasgow

Contents

	Introduction	xi
1	The Nature of Credit	1
2	Credit Information	5
	References	6
	Credit-Bureau reports	9
	Credit registers	10
	Sales-ledger information	10
	Balance sheets and other published information	13
	Direct information	15
3	Company Accounts	19
	Profit and loss account	20
	Balance sheet	22
	Auditors' certificate and balance-sheet notes	33
4	Analysis of Balance Sheets	35
	Current position	36
	Level of profits	38
	Net worth	39
	Break-up value	40

Accounts analysis form   46
Assessment of the ABC Manufacturing Company Ltd   54
Note on accounts analysis forms   59

5   Terms of Sale   60
    Monthly credit   61
    Extended credit   62
    Additional safeguards   63
    Short credit   66
    Contra accounts   69

6   Assessment and Control of Credit Accounts   72
    Assessment of new accounts   73
    Assessment of old accounts   73
    Trade disputes   82

7   Collection Procedure   85
    Terms and discounts   86
    Collection policy   87
    Collection procedure routine   88
    Some important exceptions   92
    Preparation and production of collection letters   96
    Specimen collection letters   99

8   Legal Action   110
    Collecting debts   111
    Enforcement of payment by a solicitor   113
    Legal proceedings   115
    Enforcement of judgment   117

9   Bad Debts   120
    Debtor disappears or dies   120
    Bankruptcy   121
    Liquidation of limited companies   124
    Undue or fraudulent preference   127
    Receivers   128
    Moratoriums   130
    Bad-debt provisions   132

Contents

10	**Credit Insurance**	134
	Risk factor	134
	Market intelligence	136
	Credit-insurance market	137
	Export Credits Guarantee Department	140
	Credit insurance through factoring	142
	Cost of trade-credit insurance	144
11	**Export Credit**	147
	Historical development	147
	Terms of sale	151
	Export collection procedures	156
	Export credit assessment	158
	Transfer risk	158
	Exchange risk	159
12	**The Computer as an Aid to Credit Management**	163
	What is a computer?	163
	Control section	164
	Choice of machine	167
	Credit department and the computer	168
	Open-item system	170
13	**The Credit Function**	174
	Establishing a credit policy for a company	175
	Responsibility for the credit function	176
	A credit communications network	177
14	**Organization of a Credit Department**	189
	Functions which can be delegated	190
	Functions which can be partially delegated	192
	Functions which cannot be delegated	195
	Staff training	198
Index		199

Illustrations

2:1	Trade reference letter	6
2:2	Bank reference letter	8
2:3	Sales representative's report	16
3:1	Profit and loss account of ABC Manufacturing Co. Ltd	21
3:2	Balance sheet of ABC Manufacturing Co. Ltd	24
3:3	Auditors' certificate	34
4:1	Break-up value of the ABC Manufacturing Co. Ltd	43
4:2	Accounts analysis form	44–5
4:3	Analysis of X Engineering Ltd	48–9
4:4	Analysis of Y Brothers Ltd	50–1
4:5	Break-up value of Y Brothers Ltd	53
4:6	Analysis of ABC Manufacturing Co. Ltd	56–7
6:1	Sales ledger account of Sound Traders Ltd in the books of I. M. Careful Ltd	74
6:2	Sales ledger account of Watchet & Windup Ltd in the books of I. M. Careful Ltd	76
6:3	Sales ledger account of Watchet & Windup Ltd in the books of Careless, Sellar & Co. Ltd	78
6:4	Sales ledger account of S. Low & Co. in the books of I. M. Careful Ltd	79
6:5	Sales ledger account of the Long Time Co. Ltd in the books of I. M. Careful Ltd	81

7:1   Collection procedure timetable   89
11:1   Specimen letter of credit   152
11:2   Bill of exchange payable at sight   153
11:3   Bill of exchange payable 60 days after sight   155
11:4   Bill of exchange payable on demand   157
11:5   Closing rates for foreign currencies on 2 January 1973   161
12:1   Organization chart of computerized sales-ledger function   165
12:2   Sales-ledger reconciliation   166
12:3   Computer reminder messages   170
12:4   Operation of the open-item system   171
13:1   Direct lines of communication   179
13:2   Sequence of action from receipt of a customer's order   180
13:3   Payments grading   184
14:1   Organization chart for credit department   191

Introduction

The aim of this book is to present a practical guide for the effective management of short-term trade credit. It examines some of the more common problems which face those who offer credit terms to their customers and it suggests practical methods of dealing with these problems. Also described are sources of information and its evaluation, how to establish a reasonable credit rating and, perhaps most important, how to manage a credit account after the initial evaluation has been made; this might be described as the basic technique of credit management which is sometimes neglected.

There is a tendency, even among those who take the trouble to investigate the soundness of new accounts before granting initial credit, to accept the assumption that a man or a business which is said to be creditworthy is creditworthy. There are two fallacies in this approach: first, creditworthiness is not an absolute, it is a relative term. Some firms are more creditworthy than others and each must therefore be evaluated if credit management is to be effective. Second, it assumes that businesses do not change, whereas all businesses are constantly changing. If good profits are being made the business is growing stronger, but if losses are incurred the business must be weaker as a result. It is for these reasons that the subsequent management of a credit account is even more important than the initial assessment. Good management or 'care and maintenance' will soon highlight indifferent assessment work. Mistakes in assessments, based as they are on third-party information, are unavoidable, but loss will be rare if subsequent management of the account is designed to throw up and rectify such mistakes. Good assessment work is, however, no substitute for care and maintenance since changing events will inevitably render any assessment, however carefully carried out, irrelevant, with the passage of time.

The second part of the book is concerned with collecting payment. This is sometimes regarded as a menial task, not to say a bore and an embarrassment. Customers know this as well as suppliers and some of them will not be loath to take advantage of such an attitude. Outstanding debts cost money – money which few firms can afford to do without, because it is totally unprofitable money. Collection work is less a science, more an art, because its aim is to obtain payment as quickly as possible while at the same time maintaining customer goodwill. On the other side of the coin, ineffective collection work not only costs interest, in so far as the money tied up in uncollected accounts cannot be used to meet the cost of purchases and all the other necessaries, but it directly leads to actual bad debts. There is no debt so bad as the one for which no attempt is made to collect.

Chapters 8 and 9 examine in some detail accounts which are in serious difficulties and cannot pay. Several courses of action are open to a creditor in such a situation. The aim here is again to minimize actual loss in an already unsatisfactory situation and Chapter 9 ends with some observations on making adequate provision for bad and doubtful debts.

No book on this subject would be complete without making reference to credit insurance, whereby much of the risks outlined in previous chapters can be laid off for quite modest premiums. Chapter 10 describes the types of insurance available for both domestic and export trade and how they operate.

Chapter 11 is devoted to the increasingly important subject of export credit management and Chapter 12 explores some computer applications to the general problem of sound credit management.

The last chapters are devoted to the organization and administration of a credit department and its proper role within the total function of a company. Here some study is made of the relationship between the credit function and the sales function. If friction is to be avoided, swift and satisfactory lines of communication must be established between departments. The picture of the credit man sitting in an ivory tower remote from all practical and human considerations is as common as it is erroneous. He is an integral part of the whole but, if he is not properly integrated, he will tend to draw apart to the detriment of all concerned.

General management cannot escape responsibility for such a situation developing and it is suggested that an agreed company credit policy be established and understood by all the departments involved. Thus the risk of interdepartmental acrimony is virtually eliminated and morale is kept high — the key to any successful credit sales policy.

This book does not attempt to cover the problems of retail credit — that is, credit granted to private individuals — and it is not concerned with meduim- or long-term credit or hire purchase. Although some of the tenets will have equal force in these other spheres, the techniques of management and control must differ widely and, in any case, they are more of concern to specialists engaged in those trades. However, the problems of ordinary short-term trade credit are not the problems of specialists but of most businesses, many of which have insufficient time and talent available to give them the attention they merit.

This book is not designed to enable the student to pass an examination in the theory of credit management. It is meant for the practical man who is running a business and has only a limited amount of time available for this subject. It is hoped that it may also appeal to those who are involved with the problems of managing credit and it has been written in such a way that it can be passed to any intelligent youngster who should be able to assimilate it without undue difficulty. Our aim has been to write in lay terms and eliminate professional jargon. We shall be more than pleased if we have succeeded in some small way in this aim.

CHAPTER 1

The Nature of Credit

Credit involves the provision of goods or services in exchange for payment deferred. Thus a debt is owed. If payment is made in cash at the time the goods are sold, there is no debt and the question of credit does not arise. A supplier may call for payment in advance of delivery of his goods or services. In this event the question of credit does not arise for the seller, but it does arise for the buyer who has parted with cash before he has received his purchases. Just as credit should not be given to uncreditworthy buyers, so payments in advance should not be made to uncreditworthy sellers.

Why bother with credit at all? The short answer is that without it progress would be much slower and costs of production would be greater. The provision of credit enables customers to buy when they could not otherwise do so. This means greater sales volume and thus more economic deployment of production resources, which in turn lowers the unit cost of production and engenders greater profit and/or lower sales prices.

But granting credit involves the use of financial resources. A business without capital cannot grant any credit at all unless it is able to borrow funds from somebody else such as its own suppliers or a bank. It follows that granting credit depends entirely on somebody somewhere being in possession of a stock of capital. A supplier may have accumulated and retained profits over the years which enable him to give credit to his own customers, or he may only be able to give such credit as he himself can obtain from his suppliers, or he may — and this is frequently the case — borrow from a bank or other financial institution in order to raise sufficient funds to give credit to his customers. In either case, the supplier must have resources of capital at his command if he is to give credit to his customers by parting with goods today for which he will not receive payment until a month or more has elapsed.

Capital is not only required to enable a business to give credit, it is needed to obtain the fixed assets such as buildings, machinery, or motor vehicles necessary to carry on the business; to finance stocks and work-in-progress for the duration of the manufacturing process and ofter longer; to finance the payment of weekly wages and rent; to finance selling and the many other operating costs which are incurred before the first sales revenue begins to flow back.

This capital requirement can be met in a number of different ways. Part will doubtless have been subscribed by the proprietors of the business as shares; part may be put up as loans by individuals or by financial institutions such as banks; and part may be provided by the business's own suppliers through the trade credit which they offer.

If a business is to be run properly and safely, its stock of capital must be adequate for its requirements. Some businesses do not have adequate capital and the credit manager must learn to interpret the signs which indicate to a trained eye such financial stringency. What is adequate capital? If a business is properly run it should be able to meet its day-to-day commitments as they fall due — this is the important test. The actual capital required to support a given turnover will vary according to circumstances: the amount of fixed assets required, the amount that can be raised in loans of one sort or another, the amount of credit received and granted, to name but a few. If suppliers are willing to grant two months' credit to a business which sells for settlement in seven days, then clearly the actual capital requirement will be less than in another business which has to pay promptly for its supplies but which has to offer two months' credit to its customers. A business which turns its stock over once a week requires less capital than one which turns its stock over once a quarter. Therefore, capital requirements should not be related to turnover but to the cash requirements of the business.

This does not prevent enterprising people from endeavouring to establish businesses without capital, so long as they can obtain credit from their suppliers. In such a business, the working capital is provided by the creditors. This is a potentially dangerous situation because if anything goes wrong anywhere along the line, so that sales do not turn into cash on the anticipated date, the business will be unable to meet its obligations when they fall due. This will shake the confidence of the suppliers who will press for payment of their accounts. The less prudent they have been, the more nervous will they become and they may well bring about a collapse of the business. The creditors, however, will be the only losers because they have provided all the working capital – all that there is – in the business.

There are two distinct elements in credit which are rarely properly distinguished: the *time* element and the *amount* element. Most people recognize that giving credit of £3,000 involves a greater risk than giving the same customer credit of only £1,000. They do not so readily appreciate that £3,000 on *monthly* terms may in practice be a *lesser* risk than £1,000 on ninety-day terms. The shorter the terms, the less the risk is because, in a well-ordered administration, the overdue account can be pursued that much earlier. At the same time, if the financial situation of the customer happens to be deteriorating, this will reveal itself that much sooner. The earlier that an unsatisfactory situation comes to light, the less it will have deteriorated and the sooner it can be rectified thus reducing the likelihood of loss.

The purpose of granting extended credit is, or should be, to give the customer sufficient reasonable opportunity to conclude his own sale. If credit beyond this requirement is offered it will constitute nothing less than an open invitation to the customer to employ the money owing to his supplier in some other venture or to pay some other less lenient creditor. Far more businesses fail as a result of incompetence than as a result of any deliberate dishonesty and it is the overprovision of credit to incompetents that creates the circumstances in which the seeds of failure flourish.

In establishing an effective credit administration it is therefore necessary to supervise not only the amount or quantity of credit granted but also the length of time for which it is granted. Warning bells should ring whenever situations are not in order and these bells might aptly be called the 'amount bell' and the 'time bell'. This aspect is enlarged upon in Chapter 6.

Thus credit, like many other things, is good only in moderation. Too little credit frustrates sound trade and curtails profit. Too much credit leads in turn to overtrading, an inability to meet obligations when due, a crisis of confidence and, ultimately, failure. The purpose of this book is, first, to suggest ways and means of assessing and reassessing what is the right amount of credit to grant and, second, to outline all the many courses open to a creditor to redress the various unsatisfactory situations which may arise from time to time, even though the greatest care has been taken in the first place.

CHAPTER 2

Credit Information

Before granting credit one must be satisfied that payment may be expected in full and when it is due. The direct cost of granting credit is the cost of the finance needed for the length of time it is outstanding. If goods to the value of £5,000 are sold to a customer on thirty-day terms this involves the use of £5,000 of resources for thirty days. Therefore either that sum must be borrowed from the bank or the opportunity to employ these funds elsewhere in the business is lost. In rough figures £5,000 costs £1 a day to finance at interest of 7 per cent a year and if borrowing rates are higher then the cost is even greater.

On thirty-day terms the customer is in effect receiving a present of £30. If he takes yet another month to pay, the cost becomes £60, and so on. Most businessmen realize that granting credit is a cost to their business, but how many realize the extent of the additional cost caused by overdue accounts? This is why it is important to receive not only payment for goods or services *in full* but payment *when due*.

Accurate and up-to-date information is therefore of fundamental importance. How is it obtained?

References

Trade references

The cheapest, quickest, and commonest source of information about creditworthiness is the trade reference. It is conventional — and usually adequate — to ask a new customer for two trade references. The cost is just four postage stamps plus the time taken to write the letters.

The best way to obtain trade references is to send a brief questionnaire to the referee with a stamped addressed envelope for returning it to minimize his trouble in answering. This also ensures that the right questions are answered. A specimen letter is shown in Figure 2.1.

Two trade references which both speak favourably for the amount of credit required are normally adequate for credit up to about £250 on

Private and confidential

Dear Sirs

Brightspark and Wittyman Ltd

The above-mentioned firm has given your name as a trade reference. We shall be grateful if you will answer the questions overleaf and return this to us in the prepaid envelope provided. Any information you can give will be treated in the strictest confidence.

   We thank you in anticipation of your kind assistance and shall be glad to reciprocate at any time.

Yours faithfully

I. M. Careful
Credit Department

[Reverse side]
   Highest recent payment   £ . . . .
   Terms/discount . . . .
   Payments prompt/average/slow . . . .
   Highest credit granted   £ . . . .
   How long known . . . .
   How regarded . . . .

Figure 2:1 Trade reference letter

normal trade terms. In such cases it is probably not worth while to spend more time and money on further information. However, if either reference is in any way unsatisfactory further inquiries should be made. 'Unsatisfactory' includes an inability to speak for the quoted figure (that is, a lower amount is quoted) or reference to payments being slow or discount offered not being taken.

Misleading references. A word of warning here about fraudulent trade references, which are mercifully rare. They usually take one of two forms. The first are often written in glowing terms from unknown concerns at an accommodation address. Frequently the referee is not a limited company as it is more difficult to check a trading firm than a limited company. Often the two references will bear a remarkably similar appearance although they purport to come from different places simply because the same rogue has organized them both.

The second and more difficult type to spot are genuine references that have been provided by genuine traders who are as yet unaware that the business to whom they have been giving credit has changed hands and is now run by rogues. The best way to safeguard against this possibility is to find out for certain how long the prospective customer has been in that business. Representatives should, as a matter of course, ask about changes in customers' managements and directorates and report any such changes. References are of no value if they refer to the conduct of a previous proprietor, who may have been succeeded by an out-and-out rogue.

It is wise also to assess the standing of the party giving a reference. It is unlikely that a well-known firm will provide a misleading reference and an attempt should be made to evaluate not only the text of a trade reference but also the credentials of its source.

Bank references

A second line is the bank reference, or, as bankers like to call it, a 'bankers opinion'. This is of limited value; it is based on the conduct of the bank account alone and there are many firms which behave badly towards creditors yet impeccably towards their bank manager. But even when they do not conduct their bank account properly the bank manager can scarcely be expected to report unfavourably upon his own customer. Perhaps the bank manager at that very moment is returning cheques and trying to extricate himself from an alarmingly overdrawn and possible unsecured position. In such a case he will not give a good reference but equally he will not go out of his way to give a particularly bad one.

Just about the worst bank reference is: 'Respectably constituted company but we cannot speak for your figure'. Another guarded phrase is: 'Would not enter into commitments he could not see his way to fulfil'. Such references are unsatisfactory to say the least. Going to the other end of the scale, the best bank report is just one word: 'Undoubted'. Another which may generally be relied upon is: 'Good for your figure'. Not quite so good is: 'Considered good for your figure'. If there is any more writing than this then there is probably something on the mind of the bank manager and caution becomes advisable. Further information should be obtained.

When asking for a banker's opinion best results are obtained by stating brief details of the proposed transaction, for example:

'Is – – considered good for £250 monthly credit?' or *'Is – – considered good for £5,000 credit on ninety-day bills?'*

The customer's banker cannot be expected to be much help unless he has an indication of the amount of credit likely to be involved. Moreover, it is important if, for example, the proposed sale is for £250

Private and confidential

The Manager
Carefuls Bank Limited
10 High Street
Thistown

Dear Sir

Brightspark and Wittyman Ltd

We shall be grateful if you will make inquiries on our behalf with the following bank, whether the above-named can be considered good for £ . . . .
      Bankers:

Yours faithfully

for I. M. Careful Ltd

Figure 2:2 Bank reference letter

on monthly terms, that the banker is not asked whether the customer is 'considered good for £750' simply to be on the safe side. The bank manager in question will probably give a considerably more accurate answer when confronted with the first more realistic figure.

Bank managers can also be of help in filling is some of the background about a customer. If two good trade references have been provided by a new customer but there is reason to believe the business has recently changed hands, this can probably be clarified by asking the following question: 'Is — — well established under the present management and considered good for £250 monthly credit?'

The cost of a bank report is about 25p and it can normally be obtained only through the company's own banker. The customer's banker will not respond to a direct approach unless he has specific authority from his customer to do so and, even then, this is unconventional and is not to be recommended except in very special cases. It should always be remembered that the banker is giving an opinion based on his knowledge of his customer through the operation of the bank account and the value of the reference is therefore strictly limited. A specimen letter is shown in Figure 2.2.

Credit-bureau reports

There are a number of credit information bureaux operating on both a national and a regional scale. Some are more accurate and informative than others but all seem to be rather better in some trades than others. It is therefore sensible to shop around for the best agency in relation to a particular trade or location. The cost of a report is, at the time of writing, around £1 with discounts for 'bulk buyers' and excess charges for export inquiries. These reports provide a page or two of general information, including payments performance. When important sums come in question, some information bureaux will, on request, provide special credit surveys which can cost anything from £3 to £10 depending upon the degree of research and difficulty involved. The snag about both types of report is the time delay because they normally take about ten days to arrive and they can take up to three weeks.

In urgent cases it is possible to use the telephone or telex but, although this avoids delay, it is less satisfactory as the details are limited and the cost is greater. Of course, the written report follows later but it is best to avoid having to make difficult credit decisions in a hurry. Information has not only to be obtained but weighed.

Credit registers

If inquiries are likely to run into hundreds each year, it would probably be well worth while subscribing to a register. These books contain the names of hundreds of thousands of trading concerns, both large and small, giving very basic information on each coupled with a credit rating. The rating is useful for making quick decisions on amounts of credit which are moderate in relation to the customer's business. Provided there have been no recent and important changes in a business the ratings may be relied upon to a very large extent. The exact interpretation of these ratings depends on the publisher's method of rating and it would be imprudent to lay down a general rule of interpretation. Firms which provide this service are, however, careful to explain the exact significance of their rating systems.

Suffice to say that if a new customer is shown in the register he is almost certainly in an established way of business and is probably not a fly-by-night. If the credit in question is less than, or no greater than, the rating indicates then, recent changes in circumstances apart, that amount of credit should prove to be no undue risk. Perhaps the greatest danger in relying on ratings alone is that large firms with high ratings can decline just as can their smaller brethren. Registers are usually published annually and of necessity must be a few months out of date. It is therefore possible for a company with a high rating to fail. If relatively substantial sums of credit are involved it is best to supplement the brief information in the register with a current credit report or with up-to-date trade references.

Sales-ledger information

The most important source of information is a properly kept and up-to-date sales ledger – a source often ignored by directors and managers who are too busy with production and sales to worry about book-keeping. Sales-ledger interpretation is a quite different science from book-keeping. A good interpreter may be an indifferent book-keeper, while a first-class book-keeper may not have the first glimmering about interpretation.

With a new customer there is, of course, no sales-ledger information available to interpret and it is probably because most people carry out their credit investigations before they are owed anything that they forget to use the even more valuable and first-hand credit information that accumulates before their eyes in their own sales ledgers. There are those whose views are roseate in hue, from a splendid business lunch and high-sounding talk of big contracts and fat profit margins, who, even if they looked at the sales ledger months later, would not believe its message but would find some elaborate reason to explain why the account was not in order.

Few businesses stand still — they either make profits or losses or fluctuate from year to year from one state to another. A declining business is eventually a bad credit risk. Some businesses have sufficient reserves and accumulated strength to be able to withstand losses for years before they ultimately fail and, of course, they may also turn round at any time and start making profits again. It is of only secondary importance to know whether losses are being made because of incompetence, dishonesty, or sheer bad luck. The information that is needed is whether the rot is going to stop or continue. A customer's payments performance is a most accurate means of assessing his liquidity. If his payments are prompt his liquidity is adequate and, if this is so, he is not likely to fail. Unlike a balance sheet which is a momentary photograph of a business at the close of business on one particular day sometime in the past, the sales ledger tells a serial story from week to week and month to month just as a customer's business is either improving or declining from week to week and month to month.

After the due date for payment has passed, every further day that passes without payment represents a potential deterioration in the financial strength of the customer. If a series of debts falls due on succeeding dates a pattern will emerge with the passage of time. Payments may be regularly late or the overdue gap may gradually lengthen from three weeks to six weeks to nine weeks, and so on. Round-sum payments on account — which are better than nothing — may be received. Payments may also decline in size as time passes.

All these phenomena are faithfully recorded in the sales ledger. They all indicate financial strain to say the least and potential if not actual insolvency. It is common for this pattern to appear long before anyone dreams of calling a meeting of creditors. Indeed many creditors will not trouble themselves to read the signs, dismissing the question airily with an observation like: 'I've known old Jack for years. He would never let me down. Gets a bit tight at times but a first-class chap.' Now it may be that this character assessment of Jack is correct, but, if he is running a failing business or has been squeezed by circumstances beyond his control, no one is being helped — not even Jack — by extending further unplanned credit so that when the crash comes it is bigger and louder. If Jack is going to fail anyway early steps should be taken to minimize the company's involvement in his embarrassment.

This is why it is important to read the signs in the sales ledger. Properly handled it is the finest and most reliable early warning system available to management. Prompt remedial action will not only curtail potential loss but may bring friend Jack to his senses sufficiently early for him to take remedial steps in his own business. As a result of this he may avoid becoming hopelessly insolvent and not only avoid a loss for his creditors but remain in business as a continuing source of profit to his suppliers. One is never thanked by anyone for being the largest creditor in a liquidation. The principal victim is usually past caring and the other creditors think the largest creditor is at best the biggest idiot and at worst the direct cause of the downfall.

The converse is every bit as true: the fact that payments arrive regularly on due date and full discount (if offered) is taken is a 99 per cent sure way of telling that a customer is in good financial order. Either his cash position is thoroughly sound or his overdraft arrangements with his bankers are properly conducted. If this were not so he would be unable to conduct his affairs in such an exemplary manner. It will therefore be prudent gradually to extend more credit to such a customer and to continue to observe the payments performance.

The reason why this is only a 99 per cent and not a 100 per cent indicator is that some dishonest operators have worked this out for themselves. Experienced rogues will deliberately set out to create an impression of having more than adequate financial resources by paying their initial accounts very quickly to establish a high credit standing as soon as possible. One must therefore beware of overprompt payment which is made specifically for this purpose. This is also why credit should be gradually increased to good payers rather than doubled up in leaps and bounds. The technical term for this overprompt payer who seeks to establish large and widespread credit quickly is the 'long firm'. It is usually practised in consumer goods where a quick sale at a cut price can be easily arranged. Amongst other commodities, low-priced household and electrical goods and tinned foodstuffs lend themselves more easily to this practice than goods which have to be processed or disposed of more slowly.

The all-important part that sales ledger examination plays in credit assessment should now be appreciated. This subject will come up again in Chapter 6, on assessment and control. It does, however, also belong under the heading of 'credit information' because initial assessments, which are based on hearsay, should always be revised in the light of first-hand experience. Therefore the sales ledger, although not the first source of information in time, grows to become the first source in importance as experience of an account is gained.

Balance sheets and other published information

What further sources of information can one make use of if one takes the trouble to examine them? Perhaps the most important, not mentioned so far, are the balance sheet and profit and loss accounts of prospective customers. But, as Mrs Beeton might have said: 'First catch your balance sheet'.

If a prospective customer is a public company its accounts may, for a small fee, be examined at Companies House and an abstract may be taken. The fact that a company is 'public' is no guarantee that it is 'blue chip' or even solvent. The results of inquiries from a reliable credit inquiry bureau will, however, indicate whether a public company is thriving or in difficulties. Companies House searches can therefore be confined to those which are in difficulties or those with whom one is particularly concerned. The cost of obtaining and weighing this information is greater because one must either go personally or send someone who is knowledgeable and reliable and trained in this type of work. There is nothing so useless as an incompetent search. However, the credit inquiry bureaux are prepared also to undertake searches on behalf of their clients.

There still exists a great taboo about accounts in the United Kingdom: 'Only my bank manager and my auditors see my accounts' is a time-honoured business maxim to this day. Yet in the United States anyone expecting to receive substantial credit facilities goes to the confrontation armed with his up-to-date accounts, since no one expects to obtain credit without these. It is to be expected that this trend will gradually follow in Britain, nudged along, no doubt, by the new company legislation. The fact remains that, at the time of writing, it is still looked upon as bordering on the impertinent to ask to see a prospective customer's balance sheet and accounts and this must be borne in mind and weighed before a direct approach is made for this information.

There are, of course, many aspects to balance sheet evaluation and, although this does not pretend to be a textbook on this subject, the following chapters go into more detail. However, it may be appropriate to mention here the question of registered charges and debentures and the significance, limited though it may be, of issued or paid-up capital. One should in general terms be wary of debentures and registered charges. They signify that some third party – usually a bank but sometimes a parent company – has made available a large sum of money to enable the customer to carry on his day-to-day trade. The existence of these charges enables the lender to recover all his money before the unsecured creditors are paid a penny. Further reference is made to this aspect in Chapter 9 which deals with the problems of liquidations and receiverships.

If a parent company has lent money to a subsidiary, and has a registered charge whereby it is preferred to ordinary (unsecured) trade creditors, it is only prudent to seek the guarantee of the parent company before large business is transacted with the subsidiary. If the parent company is of undoubted public standing and owns all the shares in the subsidiary there is a temptation to take the guarantee as read. This, however, is not the legal position. A parent company is no more liable for the debts of a subsidiary company with limited liability than any shareholder whose liability is limited to his share of the paid-up capital. Special care should be taken where an 'undoubted' parent company is only partly involved. Public companies have been known to 'let subsidiaries go' and have felt no moral obligation to see creditors paid at the expense of their own share-holders. It follows from this, that, quite apart from the legal position, it is far from clear what moral obligation a parent company owes to the creditors of an ailing subsidiary. The moral of this is: if in doubt about the solvency of a subsidiary, seek the guarantee of the parent.

Paid-up capital is of particular interest where companies are of recent inception. A paid-up capital of £2 means that the proprietors of the business are trusting their enterprise with £2 of their own money. It passes comprehension why they should expect third parties – trade creditors – to trust them with more. Perhaps the fact that they do is sufficient in itself. It is to be presumed, fraud apart, that if sufficient working capital is paid up the proprietors mean serious business since they stand to lose that money if the business fails. If the paid-up capital is what is euphemistically known as 'nominal' or a nominal paid-up capital – more appropriately described as derisory paid-up capital – it may mean anything or nothing. It may be a genuine business or business for fun, the maxim being: 'If it goes well I make a bomb and if it doesn't somebody else takes the rap.' From a creditor's point of view this can be translated as being on a hiding to nothing which is far from a fair trade risk. That is not to say that credit should never be extended to a £2 paid-up company – just that creditors should be quite sure what they are doing before they do it.

There are many other indirect forms of credit information to which some weight may be attached in the absence of evidence to the contrary. The very name of a company gives a smell; for instance doubts might reasonably be entertained about a company with a name such as Pan-World Exploitations Limited, which may prove to have £2 paid-up capital and no telephone number. Relatively few businesses can operate properly without either money or a telephone and the absence of both is certainly grounds for exercising caution. Yet mushroom enterprises seem to be quite successful at obtaining credit if they try hard enough.

The existence of a company's name in a trade association booklet is no guarantee of solvency but it is at least an indication that the concern is genuinely in that particular business and the inference to be drawn is favourable on balance. The fact that a company is a 'main dealer' for a nationally known company similarly indicates that it enjoys a measure of trust from at least one quarter. Telephone directories, Post Office directories, trade directories, all these give a least an inkling in this direction. The more of these tests a prospective customer passes with flying colours the more easily one can sleep at nights and the less will be lost in bad debts.

Direct information

Representatives' reports

Quite apart from making extensive inquiries of third parties some weight should be given to what salesmen or representatives see when they call on a new customer. Whilst it is bad to waste a salesman's valuable selling time in acting as a credit sleuth, he can obviously assist the business of credit assessment if he is given the right kind of guidance and encouragement. Loudly voiced generalities – such as: 'Charming man. Must do well. Got a nice place' – are of little value.

To help ensure that representatives provide valuable information it is worth the effort to design a rep's report form (see Figure 2.3). Of course the design of this form will vary widely according to the nature of the trade. However, it is useful to know about the size of the business, how long it has been established, and details of the following: its main lines; its type of location; the correct name of its proprietor(s);

```
 1  Representative's name . . . . . . . .      2 Date  . . . . . . . .
 3  New customer's full name  . . . . . . . . . . . . . . . . . . . . . . . .
 4  Address . . . . . . . . . . . . . . . . . . . . . . . . . . . . . . . . . . . . . . .
    . . . . . . . . . . . . . . . . . . . . . . . . . . . . . . . . . . . . . . . . . . . . . .
 5  Telephone number . . . . . . . . . . . . . . . . . . . . . . . . . . . . . . .
 6  How long in business . . . . . . . . . . . . . . . . . . . . . . . . . . . . .
 7  Size (number of employees) . . . . . . . . . . . . . . . . . . . . . . .
 8  Nature of business  . . . . . . . . . . . . . . . . . . . . . . . . . . . . . .
 9  Situation  . . . . . . . . . . . . . . . . . . . . . . . . . . . . . . . . . . . . . .
10  Competitors'
    lines carried . . . . . . . . . . . . . . . . . . . . . . . . . . . . . . . . . . . .
11  Nature/value of
    initial order . . . . . . . . . . . . . . . . . . . . . . . . . . . . . . . . . . . .
12  Estimated turnover capacity
    (How much of our product                                       ⎧ week
    could he reasonably sell)  . . . . . . . . £  . . . . . .  per ⎨ month
                                                                   ⎩ year
13  Whether branch or
    subsidiary of a larger
    company (state name) . . . . . . . . . . . . . . . . . . . . . . . . . . .
14  Accounts to be
    rendered to . . . . . . . . . . . . . . . . . . . . . . . . . . . . . . . . . . . .
15  Terms of sale . . . . . . . . . . . . . . . . . . . . . . . . . . . . . . . . . . .
16  General remarks . . . . . . . . . . . . . . . . . . . . . . . . . . . . . . . . .
    . . . . . . . . . . . . . . . . . . . . . . . . . . . . . . . . . . . . . . . . . . . . . .
    (name of contact) . . . . . . . . . . . . . . . . . . . . . . . . . . . . . . .
17  Referees given (a) . . . . . . . . . . . . . . . . . . . . . . . . . . . . . . .
    . . . . . . . . . . . . . . . . . . . . . . . . . . . . . . . . . . . . . . . . . . . . . .
                  (b) . . . . . . . . . . . . . . . . . . . . . . . . . . . . . . . .
    . . . . . . . . . . . . . . . . . . . . . . . . . . . . . . . . . . . . . . . . . . . . . .
```

Figure 2:3 Sales representative's report

whether it is a branch; should its accounts be rendered elsewhere, and if so where; is it well stocked; do competitors supply them; are there similar businesses in the immediate vicinity; how much can the business reasonably purchase initially and what turnover should it be able to cope with?

An intelligent answer to each of these questions will not only help to avoid bad risks but will enable a supplier to promote trade where it will sell quickest and best. It is always a mistake to oversell a new customer, however good a risk he may be. No one wants to be overstocked with slow-moving merchandise.

There is, for instance, little point in selling mink coats to a small general merchant in the Hebrides because they are unlikely to move in any quantity. He will only pay as he sells – if he sells at all. Eventually the coats will have to be taken back and they may not have improved after a protracted stay in conditions scarcely designed for their conservation.

It may be sensible to sell marmalade to this same merchant but there is no point in selling more marmalade than can be consumed by the people in the vicinity.

All this may be obvious but it is curious that, although it may be obvious in this example, it is not so obvious when a customer is located in a large centre of population. Yet exactly the same considerations may apply because of his particular street location, or because of the income bracket of his clientele, or because he is no expert at promoting a particular line. Hence, if a relatively expensive product is to be promoted in a shop which mainly sells inexpensive products, or vice versa, payments problems should be anticipated.

As payments problems cost money they should be avoided unless prices are specifically increased to cater for this anticipated cost. This is rarely worth while except when establishing a new invention or opening a new market because it is usually more profitable to sell in a market which has an established demand for the merchandise or to select a new market with care when, having made a careful study, a successful promotion of the product is likely.

There is one particular failing in representatives which is perhaps worth mentioning: the urgent requirement for a surprisingly large quantity from a new customer. The ingenuous representative may believe he has some unique flair for selling. A more critical eye will detect the possibility that the customer in this case has had his credit stopped by his regular suppliers. He urgently requires a new source in order to convert goods to cash to pay his more pressing creditors already in the queue. This situation is an all-too-commom trap for the unwary, especially since it appears to flatter both the product and the sales technique. Overenthusiasm should always be treated with a degree of caution.

CHAPTER 3

Company Accounts

It has already been mentioned that directors of what, until 1968, were exempt private companies — exempt, that is, from publishing balance sheets — have traditionally been reluctant to show these figures to their trade creditors. Under the 1967 Companies Act, however, this exemption has been abolished and all limited companies must now file their accounts at Companies House where anyone may inspect them on payment of 15p. The only way to avoid publication is to relinquish limited liability and, although some limited companies hitherto have followed this course, it seems that the majority reluctantly and probably rather tardily post their accounts off to Companies House. Thus it is increasingly possible for a supplier to obtain details of his customer's accounts and it follows that the analysis of the information available must be an increasingly important aspect of credit management.

Although sole traders and partnerships do, of course, prepare accounts, in practice the majority of accounts to be analysed will be those of the limited liability company; for the sake of simplicity reference will be to accounts of such a concern in this chapter.

The first point to check when examining a set of accounts is whether or not they have been audited. If they have been there will be a signed certificate by the auditor. The Companies Acts[1] require every

[1] There have been a number of Companies Acts over the last century: all previous such Acts were consolidated and in part amended by the 1948 Act and a further Companies Act became law in 1967. In this book the Companies Acts refer to the Companies Act 1948 and that of 1967.

B

company's books to be subjected to regular independent audit and although it can be assumed that accounts obtained from Companies House are audited this is not necessarily the case with every set produced for a creditor's inspection. Often draft accounts are prepared prior to audit and the creditor may be shown these on the grounds that there is nothing better available. Unaudited figures are of strictly limited value.

The next important point to note about the accounts is their date. A company is required to produce every year audited accounts to its members or shareholders in general meeting and this meeting should be not later than nine months after the end of the company's financial year and fifteen months from the last meeting. The accounts should be filed at Companies House not later than 42 days after the date of the general meeting. In the past, however, many companies have been much behind in the preparation of their accounts and the 1967 Companies Act does not seem to have speeded up this process.

It is, however, an old maxim that 'late accounts are bad accounts', and this more often than not turns out to be the case. A creditor's suspicions should therefore be aroused if the accounts he is shown, although audited, are seriously out of date.

Where one company (the parent company) owns shares in another (the subsidiary) the parent company is required to produce group accounts, in addition to preparing its own accounts. These usually take the form of consolidated accounts which incorporate the figures of the subsidiary. If it is required to give credit to the subsidiary, both the subsidiary's accounts and the group accounts should be scrutinized as it is quite possible for the subsidiary's figures to be strong while the group as a whole is weak (and vice versa).

The Companies Acts prescribe the minimum amount of information which must be shown in any set of accounts and require them to show a 'true and fair' view of the assets and liabilities of the company and also its profits (or losses). They must be shown in three parts: the profit and loss account, the balance sheet, and the directors' report.

Profit and loss account

A profit and loss account is a statement of the company's profit (or loss) over a financial year. If the account is shown in full it will set out the sales turnover, the gross profit arising from this turnover, the various deductions from this figure to cover overheads until the net profit (or loss) is struck. The account will also show what happened to the net profit – how much was appropriated to reserves, how much paid out in tax and dividends, and how much was carried forward into the next trading period.

A specimen profit and loss account of an imaginary company is set out in Figure 3.1.

This profit and loss account satisfies the requirements of the Companies Act but it will be noted that no information is given

	£	£
Turnover (sales less returns and allowances)		4,798,000
Trading profit for the year		205,000
After charging		
Director's remuneration	£15,000	
Depreciation	20,000	
Debenture interest	35,000	
Auditor's remuneration	3,000	
Add		
Income from investments		
Quoted	7,500	
Unquoted	32,500	40,000
Non-recurring profits, less losses		40,000
Net profit for the year, before taxation		285,000
Deduct		
United Kingdom corporation tax		105,000
Net profit for the year after taxation		180,000
Balance brought forward from previous year		10,000
Balance available		190,000
Deduct		
Transfer to debenture redemption reserve fund	45,000	
Transfer to general reserve	75,000	
Dividends paid and proposed (gross)		
Interim (paid 20 November 1972) at 5%	20,000	
Final (proposed) at 8¾%	35,000	175,000
Balance carried forward		£15,000

Figure 3:1 Profit and loss account of ABC Manufacturing Co. Ltd
Year ended 31 March 1973

regarding the cost of sales and the margin of profit. In many cases the creditor will be unable to obtain more than this legal minimum information.

Balance sheet

A balance sheet is a statement of the assets and liabilities of a company taken out at the close of business on the last day of an accounting year. For this purpose the various assets and liabilities which are, of course, constantly changing as they are bought and sold or used and worn out are momentarily frozen. The items in a company's balance sheet include:

1 Its assets — that is, everything that it owns including any claims to monies due.
2 Its liabilities to outsiders — that is, the claims of creditors on the company's resources.
3 The other liabilities — that is, the difference between items 1 and 2. This represents the interest or equity of the shareholders of the company, sometimes referred to as the company's 'net worth'.

The total of assets and liabilities must balance and it follows that

$$\text{assets} = \text{liabilities} + \text{equity}$$
$$\text{equity} = \text{assets} - \text{liabilities}$$

The balance sheet does not show whether the company is making a profit or a loss, although comparative figures for the end of the previous financial year do have to be shown.

Both the assets and liabilities of a balance sheet are classified according to how *current* they are. A current asset or liability is one which will either produce for the company a cash receipt or require the company to make a cash payment within a short period — by convention this period is usually a year. If the company is due to make more cash payments over a period than it is due to receive, it is financially weak. As will be seen shortly, one of the requirements of a healthy balance sheet is a surplus of current assets over current liabilities; such a surplus is termed *working capital.*

Before examining in detail the constituent items in a balance sheet it is necessary to say something concerning the *value* which is attributed to them. The balance sheet reduces all its various items to a valuation in terms of money. Some items are easily valued, for example, cash or a bank overdraft, and there is not too much difficulty in valuing the company's debtors or creditors – always provided the books have been properly kept. On the other hand, items such as stock or certain fixed assets are not so easy to value. Stock in a fashion trade is subject to great swings in price over a short period. Stock in the hands of a trader may be worth one price; the same goods under the auctioneer's hammer at a sale of bankrupt stock will be worth only a fraction.

Fixed assets wear out gradually and accounts therefore provide depreciation against such assets so that there will be funds available to replace them when necessary. It is of course possible for assets to wear out or become obsolete more quickly than anticipated and assets may need periodic maintenance. If the company is in financial difficulties this maintenance may be neglected and as a result the asset may not be worth as much as its written-down book value suggests.

It should always be borne in mind that every valuation may be (*a*) accurate, (*b*) inadvertently inaccurate, or (*c*) intentionally inaccurate with a view to deceiving bank managers, tax inspectors, and creditors.

Where values are intentionally inaccurate it will be appreciated that the underlying asset value may be either *greater* or *less* than the book value attributed to it – depending mainly on whether it is the bank manager or the tax inspector for whose guidance the accounts have been prepared! The creditor must form his own view of the real state of affairs behind the figures shown to him, bearing in mind that the weaker the overall state of the company the more likely is the balance sheet to overstate assets and understate liabilities.

The next two sections examine the various assets and liabilities and discuss some of the problems relating to their valuation.

Balance-sheet assets

The assets of a balance sheet are classified as 'current assets', 'fixed assets' and 'others'. The most important from the creditor's point of view are the current assets and these will be considered first. (The balance sheet of the ABC Manufacturing Company Limited is shown in Figure 3.2 and can be referred to while reading this section.)

Authorized capital

1,000,000 ordinary shares of £1	£1,000,000
1,000,000 preference shares of 50p	500,000
	1,500,000

Issued capital

300,000 ordinary shares of £1	300,000	
200,000 preference shares of 50p	100,000	
General reserve	310,000	
Profit and loss account	15,000	
Debenture redemption reserve fund	400,000	
		1,125,000

Deferred liabilities

7% mortgage debenture repayable 1975	500,000

Current liabilities

Bank overdrafts (unsecured)	325,000	
Bills payable	10,500	
Trade creditors	443,000	
Other creditors	25,000	
Dividend	35,000	
Current tax	40,000	
		878,500
		£2,503,500

Goodwill				300,000

Fixed assets	At cost or valuation	Accumulated depreciation	Book value	
Freehold buildings	300,000	–	300,000	
Leaseholds	200,000	25,000	175,000	
Machinery	350,000	100,000	250,000	
Fixtures and fittings	50,000	20,000	30,000	
Motor vehicles	15,000	9,000	6,000	
	915,000	154,000	761,000	761,000
Investments quoted (market value)			110,000	
unquoted			55,000	165,000

Current assets

Stocks and work-in-progress	850,000
Trade debtors	390,000
Other debtors and prepayments	30,000
Cash	7,500
	1,277,500
	£2,503,500

Figure 3:2 Balance sheet of ABC Manufacturing Co. Ltd
As at 31 March 1973

Cash

This is simply the amount of notes and coins in the hands of the business, with any credit balance on a current account in the company's name at the bank. This is the most liquid asset of all, and the most difficult to falsify.

Accounts receivable (debtors)

This item represents the total owing to the company in repect of (a) goods delivered to customers on credit terms but not yet paid for, and (b) various payments made by the company in advance — such as rent or rates. Sometimes the two figures are shown separately.

The accounts receivable figure may be inflated by what are in effect goods supplied on credit to shareholders or directors. Such assets may be of doubtful value but only a detailed examination of the sales ledger will show whether this is the case.

Accounts receivable constitute an important liquid asset since these are debts which should turn into cash in the near future. If they do not it can only mean that the company is selling on long credit terms or that it is incurring bad debts. An interesting test to apply in order to verify this figure is to divide it into the total sales for the year and multiply the answer by 365.

$$\frac{\text{accounts receivable}}{\text{annual sales}} \times 365$$

= average number of days credit given to customers

This will show the average credit given to customers measured as so many days. If the answer seems excessive, by comparison with the normal custom of the trade, it is possible that this figure contains sizeable items that are moving slowly or, worse still, not moving at all! The same calculation can be applied to the previous year's figures and the results compared.

Stocks

These are materials purchased in the way of trade for resale, possibly after treatment in some way, at a profit — if all goes well. How they are constituted will depend on the nature of the business. In a manufacturing company they will be divisible into raw materials, work in progress, and finished goods. In, for example, a retail business they may simply consist of finished goods purchased for resale.

Stocks and work-in-progress are a most important item in a balance sheet since *(a)* they are likely to be one of the larger current assets and *(b)* their level is one of the factors which determine the company's profits.

Gross profit consists of the difference between net sales and the cost of goods sold, that is – after allowing for direct factory and labour costs – the sum of opening stock plus purchases, less closing stock. If the closing stock is overvalued in relation to opening stock it will be seen that profits will be correspondingly overstated, while the converse is equally true.

Overvaluation of stocks, therefore, will give a false picture of not only the balance sheet but also the profit and loss account. If this fictitious profit is then drawn out of the company by way of directors' remuneration, the position is serious indeed.

Having said this, however, accurate valuation of stock is no easy matter: fashions can change almost overnight and stock can become almost worthless. This hazard is not confined to the fashion trade but applies in some degree to stocks of finished or semi-finished goods when demand has fallen off because of changes in taste or because the design is obsolete. Quite apart from the fashion question, the season can greatly affect prices and hence values. A stock of turkeys will, for instance, be worth far more on 1 December than one month later. Thus although there may be no change in either quantity or quality there can be a marked change in value.

The current best practice for auditors with regard to their verification of the stock figure is not only to attend the physical stock-taking but also to test the various values attributed to the individual items. It is an unfortunate fact that a great many auditors still do not consider that they need do more than accept a certificate from the directors about the stock valuation, and few take any part in its physical verification. A prospective creditor should therefore bear in mind the possibility – and with a small business the distinct likelihood – that the auditors may not have themselves verified the stock figure. As a rough and ready rule, where the stock figure is shown 'as certified by directors' it almost certainly has not been verified by the auditors. Where the basis of the valuation is disclosed 'at the lower of cost or net realizable value' then, in the absence of suspicious circumstances, it is reasonable to assume that the stock has been properly verified by the auditor.

It follows that, when examining a balance sheet, it is important to find out as much as possible regarding the valuation of stocks and work-in-progress and a prospective creditor should view a large increase in this figure over a year with a certain amount of caution.

One way to help establish whether or not a stock valuation is likely to be accurate is to measure the figure against other indicators in the accounts. For instance, is the business expanding and thus justifying larger stocks? Have substantial profits been made and declared? If so, it is less likely that the directors will have deliberately overvalued the stock, thus obliging the company to pay even more tax. Second, a general knowledge of conditions of recession or boom, surplus or scarcity, obsolescence or modernity, will help in the task of assessing whether or not a stock valuation is surprisingly high or low. A creditor should be in a position to recognize an abnormal situation and having done so should seek a rational explanation. If there is none it is likely that the stock figure is unreliable and, even if it is not, if it is too high or too low in relation to the business requirements this reflects poor management.

There are a number of practical tests which can be applied to the stock figure. The best of all is the following formula:

$$\frac{\text{stocks}}{\text{annual purchases}} \times 365$$

= average number of days purchases represented by stocks.

This ratio can be compared with what is usual in the trade concerned and with the figure for the previous year. This is particularly useful where the manufacturing process is a simple one. It is of less value when applied, for example, to a contractor who may have months or even years of work-in-progress in his balance sheet.

The figure for purchases may not be available and if this is the case the stock figure can be measured against the figures for sales. This is a less precise measurement since stock *should* be valued on a cost basis and the sales figure will include a profit mark-up but if the calculation is made for more than one year it will show whether or not the stock figure is tending to increase.

A comparison over three years or so of the relationship between the stock figure and debtors can be of great significance and this point is referred to in more detail in Chapter 4.

Investments and loans

Separate figures for quoted and unquoted investments must be shown in the balance sheet. If an investment is quoted the market value must be shown. If it is unquoted then it may appear at a director's valuation or there may be information regarding the profits arising from the investment. Whether these items should be considered current assets or not depends on the repayment terms.

Large industrial companies periodically hold Treasury bills or make cash deposits with local authorities; such investments are current assets. A loan to an associate company, if repayable within twelve months of the balance sheet date, is technically a current asset but should not be considered as such if it is thought that the associate company will be unable to repay on time. To evaluate such a figure it may be necessary to investigate the associate company in its turn. Loans and investments if not repayable in twelve months are deferred assets and should not be included in the total of current assets.

Formation expenses

When a company is formed the costs of its formation are sometimes written off over a number of years. The part which has not been written off is shown in the balance sheet as an asset although it should not be considered as such in any kind of analysis as it is of no tangible value.

Goodwill

The goodwill of a company has been defined as: 'Nothing more than the probability that the old customers will revert to the old place'. Goodwill is difficult to value. It is not usually shown in a balance sheet unless it represents part of a payment made to acquire the assets, including goodwill, of a previous business. A prudent businessman will usually write off goodwill out of profits as quickly as possible. For the purpose of financial analysis any goodwill figure should be deducted from net worth to arrive at net tangible worth (page 39).

Patents, trade marks, etc

These are self-explanatory and, like goodwill, should be speedily written out of profits as a matter of sound financial policy. If they are shown in the balance sheet as an asset they should be deducted from net worth for the purposes of analysis.

Fixed assets

These are largely self-explanatory, representing those assets of the company which are held, not for the purpose of resale but to enable the business to be carried on. They include freeholds, leaseholds, buildings, machinery, fixtures and fittings, and motor vehicles. Fixed assets may be shown either at cost or at valuation, but in either case depreciation will also be shown provided up to the date of the balance sheet, as in the following example:

Freehold buildings at cost   £100,000
Less depreciation to 31 December 1973   10,000 = £90,000

So far as the prospective creditor of the company is concerned the most interesting points to be examined are the degree to which these assets have been written down and whether they contain a substantial break-up value. If the depreciation shown is high this is a good sign and indicates that the company has followed a prudent and conservative policy, since the amounts provided as depreciation over the years reduce the amount of profit available for distribution. The actual value of these assets is also of interest as this will give an indication of what they will realize in a liquidation. (See the section on break-up values on page 40.)

Balance-sheet liabilities

These items cover all claims on the company on the one hand from outsiders, and on the other hand by the shareholders or *members* of the company. Liabilities can be classified into:

1   Current liabilities (payable within 12 months).
2   Deferred liabilities (payable after minimum of 12 months).

3   The balance – sometimes known as the equity or the proprietor's interest in the business.

Items 1 and 2 above are liabilities to persons outside the company and item 3 is due to the members of the company and represents their investment in the company.

Creditors and accrued charges

The figure for trade creditors shows the sum of monies owing by the company in respect of its purchases of goods and services in the way of trade, that is, the goods which, having been purchased, have become part of the stock item on the assets side of the balance sheet but have yet to be paid for. This item usually includes associated charges such as carriage inwards.

Sometimes an item of 'bills payable' will be shown. This covers bills of exchange accepted in respect of purchases of goods. Historically most purchases of goods on credit were made by means of bills, but their use has declined considerably in home trade since the beginning of the century although they are still commonplace in international trade. Bills payable can be regarded, therefore, as another form of trade creditor.

It is interesting to compare the sum of trade creditors and bills payable with the figure for trade debtors on the assets side of the balance sheet and to see whether the business is a net taker or giver of credit. Other things being equal the company is in a much stronger position if it is a net giver of trade credit and it should particularly be remembered that the debtors figure includes an element of profit margin not present in the figure for creditors.

If the figure for purchases is available the following formula will calculate the average number of days' credit taken from suppliers:

$$\frac{\text{trade creditors plus bills payable}}{\text{annual purchases}} \times 365$$

= average number of days credit taken from suppliers

It will be appreciated that the figure for purchases is not the same as that of sales turnover and the purchases figure may not be shown.

Sometimes an item 'other creditors and accrued charges' is shown. This covers other sums due from the business in respect of goods and services other than those required strictly for the purpose of trade. This item might cover purchases of capital goods, although these items sometimes find their way into the trade creditor's figure. There is no particular significance in whether or not trade or other creditors are shown separately.

Bank loans and overdrafts

For these to be current liabilities, repayment must technically be due within twelve months. If the bank has taken security over any assets of the company this should be stated in a note to the balance sheet. It cannot be assumed however that the overdraft is unsecured if no such note is shown since the bank may have taken security from the directors by way of guarantees or charges on their personal property. In this case no mention of security will be made in the company's accounts.

Current taxation

Any tax charge payable within twelve months must also be included among current liabilities. If the tax is payable after twelve months it should be regarded as a deferred liability.

Proposed dividends

Once the payment of a dividend has been declared by the company in general meeting it becomes a liability of the company until paid and it must therefore be shown as a current liability.

Directors' loans

These are monies lent to the company by its directors but which are technically repayable at short notice. In practice they may arise where a director does not draw the full salary, commission, or other fee which is due to him. With small companies whose issued capital may be a purely nominal figure, directors' loans may be substantial.

A delicate question of assessment arises in cases where a company is reliant for its survival upon directors' loans. If, for instance, the company were to be put into voluntary liquidation, the directors' loan would have the same priority for repayment as the ordinary trade creditors, whereas the same funds employed in the business as paid-up capital would rank *behind* ordinary trade creditors.

As a general rule, large credit should not be extended to companies with a small or nominal paid-up capital and large directors' loans. Either the directors should be asked to convert the loan into capital (see 'Share capital and reserves' below) or they could be invited to sign an exchange of letters undertaking to 'stand back' – that is, in the event of failure not to claim any dividend until the outside creditors' claims have been satisfied in full. The company itself should be a party to this exchange of letters.

Other loans

Generally the date and terms on which other loans are repayable will be shown and this is of interest to the creditor. As with a bank overdraft, if any security has been given by the company this should be mentioned either in the actual balance sheet or as a note attached.

It should be remembered that long-dated loans become short dated upon liquidation and if they are debentures they then rank in front of other creditors.

Share capital and reserves

It has already been shown that the capital and reserves – or proprietors' equity – must be equivalent to the total of the assets less liabilities to outsiders. The capital and reserves thus represent what is left after outside liabilities have been set off against the available assets. The Companies Acts strictly regulate what may or may not be done with these items.

Two figures will be shown for share capital – authorized and issued capital. Authorized capital has little significance for the creditor who should concentrate on the issued capital. This latter is the total of shares which the company has issued to its members (shareholders). Whether the shares are of large or small denomination is also of no account, it is the total value which matters. The description or class of share – that is, whether they are ordinary, A ordinary, preference, or cumulative preference – is also relatively unimportant to a creditor since these terms merely describe the rights of the holders of the different classes of share.

The fundamentally important point about the total of the share capital is that this sum has been put into the company by the members and in any liquidation their claim on the available assets is subordinated to all other creditors. Other things being equal, the larger the share capital therefore the safer are the creditors. Moreover the Companies Acts prohibit the removal of this capital from the company except on terms which ensure the safety of the creditors.

Reserves are slightly different, they arise in two ways. The share capital may have been issued to members at a price in excess of its par value – that is, at a premium. Any such premium must be credited to a share premium account and shown separately among the reserves. The creditors can safely regard this share premium account as part of the company's share capital. The other form of reserve arises from profits which have been earned over the years and ploughed back into the business instead of being paid out as dividends, tax, or directors' remuneration. Such reserves can broadly be divided into capital reserves and revenue reserves. As these names suggest, capital reserves are held to safeguard the shareholders' capital investment (for example should it be necessary to write down the value of certain assets as the result of some calamity), and revenue reserves are held to enable the company to continue paying dividends although temporarily not trading at a profit.

Sometimes the reserve is termed a general reserve in which case it can be used for either purpose. The undistributed balance on profit and loss account is in effect a general reserve.

It follows therefore that reserves do not provide quite the same security to a creditor as does issued share capital but they are nevertheless important as they do strengthen the company. A creditor seeing substantial reserves built up in a balance sheet can safely assume that prudent policies have been followed by the directors in the past and may assume that these policies are unlikely to change in the near future – provided of course that the directors themselves have not changed. If there has been a change in control, the creditor should be aware of this, through his Companies House search or his status report, and he will have to decide on the facts available what effect this change will have on the company's financial policies.

Auditors' certificate and balance-sheet notes

In addition to the main items in a balance sheet there are also the auditors' certificate and a number of additional notes.

Report to the members of the ABC Manufacturing Company Ltd
In our opinion the accounts on pages 4–8 comply with the Companies Acts 1948 and 1967 and give so far as concerns members of the company a true and fair view of the state of affairs of the company at 31 March 1973 and of the profit of the company for the year ended on that date.

Tickit and Vouch
Chartered accountants

Figure 3:3 Auditors' certificate

Auditors' certificate

It has already been pointed out that the accounts of all limited companies must be audited. Having completed his investigation, the auditor will sign a certificate for inclusion in the balance sheet. A typical certificate is shown in Figure 3.3. It is *most* important to read this certificate carefully.

Notes to the balance sheet

The balance sheet will also contain various notes. These may contain information concerning various items, giving, for example, the basis on which they have been valued, details of any charges given by the company as security to creditors, and details of contingent liabilities. They should be read and their import carefully considered.

CHAPTER 4

Analysis of Balance Sheets

Chapter 3 reviewed the main items to be found in a balance sheet and profit and loss account of a limited company. The next question to be considered is how these many different items can be analysed to distinguish a strong or a weak situation. Before discussing this subject in detail there are certain general points to consider. Broadly speaking, balance-sheet analysis consists of:

1 Comparing the magnitude of different items in the same set of accounts to see what the *actual position* was at a given date.
2 Comparing identical items in different sets of accounts to see what the *trend* was over a period of time. When looking at the trend it is best to take a minimum of three years' figures to allow for any temporary divergence from the underlying tendency.

For the sake of brevity the following paragraphs concentrate on the comparison of different items in the same accounts. At each stage, however, the analyst should compare the latest figures with those for previous years to show whether the underlying position is improving or deteriorating.

Commerce is too frequently faced with apparently strong concerns failing, but in most cases a careful analysis of the *trend* of the various ratios outlined would at least have warned the creditors of possible trouble ahead. Two companies might have apparently similar positions at a given date, but if one had declined to that position over the previous six years and the other improved to that position then the different trends not only call for a different appreciation of the future but also for a mental valuation of the assets that is different from the figures shown in the balance sheet. To say the least, there is little pressure on the upward-moving company to overstate its assets or forget liabilities and thereby pay more tax than it has to.

At this point readers may think that they are becoming increasingly bewildered by a mass of detail. At least half the art of balance-sheet analysis consists of simplifying the mass of information available and producing it in a readily digestible manner. A useful form designed to help the analyst simplify the picture a good deal and highlight the most important points is shown in Figure 4.2. Before describing this form and its use it is necessary first to examine the four principal aspects of a company's accounts – (*a*) the current position, (*b*) the level of profits, (*c*) the net worth, and (*d*) the break-up value.

Current position

The current position is a comparison of current assets with current liabilities; it provides a very real measure of the liquidity of the company. Earlier it was shown that current assets include cash, debtors and stock, while current liabilities are those falling due within one year of the balance-sheet date, including creditors, bills payable, short-term loans, and bank overdrafts.

A liquid balance sheet is one containing a healthy surplus of current assets over current liabilities – sometimes referred to as a healthy working capital. Such a company will have little difficulty in meeting the claims on its resources as they fall due, since those same resources are producing cash equally quickly or perhaps even more quickly than are the claims.

Of all the tests which can be applied to a balance sheet, the size of the current ratio is the most important.

$$\text{current ratio} = \frac{\text{current assets}}{\text{current liabilities}}$$

From the creditors' point of view a current ratio of 2 (or £2 current assets to each £1 of current liabilities) is a strong ratio. A ratio of 1 is far from strong and a ratio of less than 1 is verging on the dangerous. It will be noted that the ABC Manufacturing Company Limited has a current ratio of 1.5 which, while not overliquid, appears to be reasonably satisfactory.

However, the needs of one business will differ from those of another and although a current ratio of 1.5 may be adequate for one it may be rather tight for another. For instance, in a business where the purchase terms are 14 days and the sales are 60 days, a higher current ratio will be needed than where the situation is the other way about.

While still considering the current ratio and the current position, another test is to make the same calculation but exclude the stock from the assets. This provides the liquid ratio:

$$\text{liquid ratio} = \frac{\text{current assets minus stock}}{\text{current liabilities}}$$

Chapter 3 (page 26) has already described the difficulty of evaluating the stock figure and the fact that the stock may possibly not be the subject of firm orders and prove difficult to turn into cash. By excluding the stock altogether a stricter measurement of liquidity is obtained.

A liquid ratio of 1 (£1 liquid asset to £1 current liabilities) is very good. A ratio of less than 0.5 should prompt questions about the extent to which the total stocks are the subject of firm orders and will therefore shortly turn into debtors and thence cash.

Another way of looking at the same problem is to calculate the ratio of stock to debtors in successive accounts:

$$\text{debtor/stock ratio} = \frac{\text{debtors}}{\text{stock}}$$

It is not usually a good sign if the proportion of stock is increasing. It is quite possible for an improvement in the current ratio to be entirely the result of an increase in stocks. In fact this would not normally be considered an improvement at all but rather the reverse unless there were known to be good reasons for the higher stock figure.

The ABC Manufacturing Company has a liquid ratio of 0.5 which is only barely satisfactory and emphasizes the importance of the stock.

Level of profits

A company which is making healthy profits is not likely to fail. Having examined the current position, the analyst should turn next to the profit and loss account.

It is important to consider the gross profit margin – that is, profit before interest, selling expenses, depreciation, etc. Clearly a company earning a gross profit of £20,000 on turnover of £500,000 is in a less healthy position than one with the same gross profit earned on a turnover of £100,000. Formerly the figure for turnover was frequently not shown in the accounts but, since the 1967 Companies Act, sales turnover is required to be shown and shown, moreover, broken down into different classes of business.

Whether a given margin of profit is healthy or not depends on the trade. For most manufacturers a gross margin of 25 to 30 per cent would be adequate but a wholesaler might will flourish with a margin of 12 to 15 per cent. A manufacturer must, from his gross profit, finance depreciation on expensive plant and machinery and possibly carry heavy stocks. The wholesaler or merchant will in contrast have relatively low overheads. In short, the gross profit figure must be compared with what is known to be a fair return in the trade concerned.

The ABC Manufacturing Company had a net profit of £285,000 before tax but the gross profit ratio was only 5.8 per cent. The accounts shown in Figures 3.1 and 3.2 are in fact, the minimum required by the Companies Acts: 'gross profit' is taken after interest and administrative and selling expenses have been deducted. In most cases the prospective creditor will have no fuller figures than these on which to base his credit judgement.

As mentioned above, the profit and loss account shows how the gross profit is accounted for. For the analyst there are two particular point to note:(a) How much of the profit is retained in the business (retentions)? and (b) what is the total of retained profit plus depreciation (cash flow)?

The amount of retentions – that is, retained profit – after providing for all expenses, charges, dividends, and tax, represents the increase in the net worth of the company as a result of its exertions throughout the financial year. This change in net worth may, in fact, be a negative figure if the gross profit has been insufficient to cover the various deductions or if the directors have drawn out more in dividends and fees than the company has earned. The analyst will, however, hope to find that a reasonable balance has been either retained as the undistributed balance on profit and loss or, alternatively, has been transferred to reserves. It will be seen the the ABC Manufacturing Company's retentions total £125,000.

The 'cash flow' is the total of retentions plus depreciation. The amount of depreciation is almost as important in this context as the amounts of retentions. Depreciation is a charge on profits which is retained in the business to offset the wasting value of fixed assets. If it were not necessary to replace theses fixed assets in the fullness of time, the depreciation figure could be added to profits; the cash flow figure is thus another measure of the company's immediate liquidity. In the example of the ABC Manufacturing Company, cash flow amounts to £145,000.

The prospective creditor may have been somewhat concerned to find that his customer has been distributing fully all earnings but if, in fact, there is a high depreciation charge, the creditor can to some extent be reassured that the divident distribution policy is not, in fact, draining the company of all fresh cash resources. Indeed, with large quoted companies, when the time comes to scrap and replace the assets on which the depreciation has been provided, their dividend records may enable them to finance this capital expenditure through a fresh issue of shares or by means of deferred indebtedness, leaving the current position unchanged.

Net worth

The net worth of a company (total assets minus liabilities to outsiders) is the same as the sum of the company's capital and reserves; but among the assets may be included certain intangible items, notably goodwill, and it is thus possible for a company to show a substantial net worth by including a large figure of goodwill among the assets. When considering the net worth of a company it is therefore more prudent to exclude such intangibles and work on the basis of net tangible worth.

The creditor will hope to find that net tangible worth is increasing over the years. One of the most dangerous signs of all is declining net worth.

Another important ratio to calculate is the borrowing ratio or ratio of total borrowing to net tangible worth. For the purpose of this calculation, creditors are not regarded as part of the borrowing although, if this figure is rather high, it must be borne in mind that there is an element of borrowing here. Although this ratio may not be much help when considering a small concern it is a useful test to apply to large companies whose assets may be vast but who may be heavily in debt to their bankers and, therefore, trading on a narrow base.

Whether a given borrowing ratio is excessive or not depends on the nature of the business. For a manufacturing company, a borrowing ratio of 50 to 60 per cent of net tangible worth is quite sound but a ratio of 100 per cent is rather high. A wholesaler, on the other hand, could in many cases trade safely with a borrowing ratio of around 100 per cent.

Property companies have higher ratios, but are very much special cases and have little need for trade credit.

For a large well-established finance company which has very small fixed assets and no stock, a borrowing ratio of six times net tangible worth is not unusual and in practice such companies may have even higher borrowing ratios.

The net worth of a company can be likened to the cushion on which the creditors sit. If it is small in relation to total liabilities the creditors may have an uncomfortable journey in front of them.

Break-up value

Up to this point the balance sheet has been considered on the basis of the company as a going concern. One form of analysis, however, is to give to the various items the value that they might be expected to fetch in a liquidation. This is a popular method with some analysts but it should not be overrated, unless the profit and loss account or declining liquidity over a period indicates the possibility of impending liquidation. To be on the safe side when using this form of analysis, it must be assumed that the company is going into liquidation and the various assets must therefore be heavily written down.

Inevitably this method is largely based on guesswork, for it is difficult to forecast what different assets will fetch under the hammer. Furthermore there is a definite tendency for accounts produced by a company which is in difficulties to show a rather better position than in fact is the case. Most companies which fail have been badly managed and the prudent creditor must make allowances for the fact that this bad management may have extended to the book-keeping. Having said this, the 'break-up' approach does provide a useful check on the impressions formed from studying the current position, profits, and net worth. If the impression formed from these earlier studies is poor, and analysis of the break-up value confirms these impressions, there is little doubt that the proposed credit should be avoided.

The usual way to construct this analysis is to prepare a list of assets, showing opposite each one its estimated break-up value, and then to deduct the liabilities. In this calculation any secured indebtedness should be set off in full against the assets charged; the balance of the realizable assets should then be compared with the remaining liabilities. If there remains a surplus all is well; if not the analyst can even try to forecast the dividend which will be paid in a liquidation!

The following comments are a guide to how each item should be valued.

Valuation of assets

Cash. This can be valued at 100 per cent of book value.

Debtors. These should realize a good proportion of their book value, say 80 to 85 per cent, unless there is any reason to believe otherwise. If, for example, it is thought that there is not a good spread of names, or if this item is turning slowly, the break-up value should be reduced accordingly. Prepayments, if they are shown separately, will not, of course, realize anything in a liquidation. Accounts in respect of goods sold to directors or their families may also be of no value.

Stock. This is a difficult item to value and a great deal depends on the trade. Fashion or novelty goods are, for example, worth practically nothing in a forced sale. If stock is high in relation to the total assets, the greatest possible care should be exercised. A conservative valuation would be 25 per cent and anything over 50 per cent of book value would be on the high side.

Investments. Quoted investments, if valued at market price, should realize close to 100 per cent of the book value.

Unquoted investments and loans to associate companies or to directors will have to be assessed in the light of information available.

Motor vehicles. The value of these is not usually great in a liquidation. There may be hire-purchase contracts running and the vehicles will thus be liable to be repossessed by the finance company. Perhaps 20 per cent of the book value should be shown as a reasonable figure.

Fixtures and fittings. The value of these items is problematical. 20 per cent of book value is a reasonably prudent estimate.

Machinery. Unless something is known of the type and age of the machinery in question valuation of this item is very much a matter of guesswork. Like motor vehicles, the machinery may be leased or held on hire purchase and thus liable to be repossessed. Depending on circumstances, anything between 20 and 50 per cent may be a reasonable expectation.

Leasehold property. This may be of considerable value if the position and condition of the buildings is good. If maintenance has been neglected, however, a lease may cost more than it is actually worth before it can be disposed of. Its value will also depend on the time it has to run, the rent payable, and the restraints or covenants if any.

Freehold property. This will probably be worth at least its book value, having regard to price trends in recent years, unless there is reason to believe that the valuation is on the high side or that the buildings are in a very dilapidated state.

Valuation of liabilities

Whether these are current or long term they must be computed at full book value – although it is not unknown for creditors of an ailing company to be understated and this possibility should be borne in mind.

Calculation of break-up value

The total of any secured liabilities including debentures should be set off at full book value against the estimated realizable value of the assets on which they are secured leaving a balance to be applied against the claims of the unsecured creditors. If the remaining assets are sufficient

	Book value	Estimated to realize
Cash (100%)	£7,500	£7,500
Debtors (80%)	420,000	336,000
Stocks and work-in-progress (33%)	850,000	283,000
Investments: quoted (100%)	110,000	110,000
unquoted (75%)	55,000	41,000
Motor vehicles (20%)	6,000	1,200
Fixtures and fittings (20%)	30,000	6,000
Machinery (50%)	250,000	125,000
Leaseholds (75%)	175,000	132,000
Freehold buildings (100%)	300,000	300,000
Goodwill	300,000	
	£2,503,500	£1,341,700
Less: Secured creditors Trustees of 7% mortgage debentures	500,000	500,000
	2,003,500	841,700
Unsecured creditors	£878,500	£878,500
	Deficiency	£36,800

Figure 4:1 Break-up value of the ABC Manufacturing Co. Ltd

to cover the balance of liabilities it is clear that the company will be able to pay 100p in the £ to its unsecured creditors.

The balance sheet of the ABC Manufacturing Company has been analysed by this method in Figure 4.1. It would appear from this calculation that, in fact, the ABC Manufacturing Company Limited would be unable to pay a dividend of 100p in the £ to unsecured creditors, although examination of the current position, profits, and net worth disclosed a reasonably satisfactory situation. This estimated deficiency mainly reflects the heavy stock position which was also to be seen from examination of the current position.

The fact that analysis of the break-up value suggests that the company is insolvent while examination of the current position, profits, and net worth indicated that the company was no worse than rather illiquid, highlights the difficulty in using the break-up value method. The assets *must* be heavily written down if this method is not to mislead dangerously but if the company is trading reasonably satisfactorily there is no reason to anticipate liquidation and therefore no need to write down the assets.

PART 1 FINANCIAL SUMMARY

Company
Auditors

Audited accounts dated			
Position as at			
Period (if other than 12 months)			

1   Net current assets (36 − 49)
2   Current ratio (36/49%)
3   Net tangible worth
      (beginning of period)
  (a) Add/deduct retentions
  (b) Add/deduct
  (c) Add/deduct
4   Net tangible worth
      (end of period)
5
6 Gross profit ratio (%)			

7 Sales (for period) 8 Purchases			

9   Gross profit
10 (a) Less overhead expenses
  (b) Less depreciation
  (c) Less directors' fees
11   Trading profit (9 − 10)
12   Other income
13   Other expenditure
14   Net profit before tax
15   Less taxation
16   Net profit after tax (14 − 15)
17   Dividends
18 Retentions			

19 Cash flow			

Notes

Figure 4:2 Accounts analysis form

PART 2 BALANCE-SHEET ANALYSIS

Position as at

Fixed assets
20 Land and buildings (net)
21 Plant and equipment (net)
22 Others (net)

23 Total fixed assets

Miscellaneous assets
24 Investments (unquoted)
25 Investments/loans to associates
26
27

28 Total miscellaneous assets

Current assets
29 Cash
30 Investments (quoted)
31 Trade debtors
32 Other debtors
33 Stock and work-in-progress
34
35

36 Total current assets

37 Total assets (excluding intangibles)

Current liabilities
38 Due to banks (secured)
39 Due to banks (unsecured)
40 Bills payable

41 Trade creditors
42 Other creditors
43 HP commitments
44 Current tax
45 Dividend
46 Current loans
47
48

49 Total current liabilities

Deferred liabilities
50 Mortgages
51 Loans (long dated)
52 Future tax

53 Total deferred liabilities

54 Total outside liabilities

Shareholders' funds
55 Issued capital
56 Capital reserves
57 P and L account
58 Other revenue reserves

59 Total shareholders' funds

60 Less intangibles

61 Net tangible worth

62 Total liabilities
   (excluding intangibles)

45

Accounts analysis form

Figure 4.2 shows a form on which the accounts of any limited company can be quickly broken down and analysed. The student of balance sheets should become thoroughly familiar with this form or with a similar one and should practise analysing accounts, since by this means he will learn more about balance-sheet analysis than from merely reading textbooks.

The analysis form is in two parts: part 2 which has to be completed first consists of an analysis of the balance-sheet figures; part 1, entitled 'financial summary', consists of an extract of the profit and loss account and a summary of the main ratios which highlight the strength or weakness of the subject of the analysis. In the illustration there are a sufficient number of columns for a comparative analysis of three years' accounts on the same form. To begin with a minimum of three years' figures should be analysed. If the form is to be used for a continuous analysis of a customer then extra columns should be provided. The form can then be filed away ready for successive years' figures to be added as they become available. Throughout the form under the various headings there are spare lines available for use as required. These spare lines should not be used unless necessary as it is desirable to keep the overall picture as simple as possible.

Part 2, the 'balance-sheet analysis', is quite straightforward to complete. It will be seen that fixed assets are classified into land and buildings, plant and equipment, and others. All are shown net of depreciation.

It will be noted that 'quoted investments' are shown under 'current assets'. It may, however, be preferable to show such investments under the 'miscellaneous' heading if there is any doubt about their ready marketability. Due to banks (secured) or (unsecured) also requires a word of explanation. The bank loan in question should be shown as secured only if it is secured on assets of the company. If outside security has been given (that is, directors' guarantees) then so far as the company is concerned the loan is unsecured. (The analyst or prospective creditor will nevertheless still be keenly interested to see whether the bank considers the company strong enough to be financed on an unsecured basis.) It will be noted that intangibles are not included as assets but are deducted from net worth to produce net tangible worth. Finally, item number 62 — total liabilities (excluding intangibles) — must of course agree with number 37 — total assets (excluding intangibles) – and is provided merely to check the arithmetic of the compiler.

Part 1 – the financial summary – falls into three sections. The first section is a list of the key indicators of the company's financial strength: net current assets, the current ratio, net tangible worth at the beginning and end of each period, and the ratio of gross profit to turnover. The next section shows total purchases (this figure may well not be available) and total sales which, since the 1967 Companies Act, must now be published. The third section is an analysis of the profit and loss account.

Item 10*a* may not be available in which case the gross profit figure (9) will be shown after deduction of overhead expenses. It all depends on the detail which is provided in the profit and loss account. Depreciation (10*b*) and directors' fees (10*c*) must be shown, however, and any income and expenditure which are not a direct result of the company's trading must also be shown separately in the published accounts (items 12 and 13). This then produces the most important figure of all – profit before tax (14). The remainder of this section shows to what purpose this profit (or loss) has been applied – tax, dividends, or retentions. Cash flow, as mentioned earlier, is merely the sum of retentions and depreciation.

Before leaving discussion of this form to look at some practical examples, it should perhaps be emphasized that there is nothing magic about it. It is designed to simplify the available figures, tabulate them in logical order, and compare successive years' accounts so that the trend is clearly visible. Not all balance sheets are particularly clearly set out and the use of a form such as this should help in highlighting the more important features.

Examples of use of the accounts analysis form

The use of this analysis form is demonstrated by practical examples in Figures 4.3 and 4.4. First, X Engineering Limited, who manufacture a certain patented machine. The company appears to be trading satisfactorily. The current ratio has been 131%, 137%, 147%, but this has been on a rising turnover and the actual surplus of current assets has risen over the three-year period from £80,000 to £182,000. It is noteworthy that until recently the company has been taking more credit than it has been giving and the creditors are to some extent financing the stock.

PART 1 FINANCIAL SUMMARY (£'000)

Company *X Engineering Limited*
Auditors *Tickit & Vouch*

Audited accounts dated	*March 71*	*March 72*	*April 73*
Position as at	*31-12-70*	*31-12-71*	*31-12-72*
Period (if other than 12 months)			
1 Net current assets (36 − 49)	*80*	*111*	*182*
2 Current ratio (36/49%)	*131*	*137*	*147*
3 Net tangible worth (beginning of period)	*180*	*190*	*212*
(a) Add/deduct retentions	*+10*	*+22*	*+38*
(b) Add/deduct			
(c) Add/deduct			
4 Net tangible worth (end of period)	*190*	*212*	*250*
5			
6 Gross profit ratio (%)	*10.4*	*12.6*	*16.0*
7 Sales for period	*800*	*915*	*1,080*
8 Purchases			
9 Gross profit	*83*	*115*	*172*
10 (a) Less overhead expenses			
(b) Less depreciation	*16*	*15*	*25*
(c) Less directors fees	*10*	*10*	*30*
11 Trading profit (9 − 10)	*57*	*90*	*117*
12 Other Income			
13 Other expenditure			
14 Net profit before tax	*57*	*90*	*117*
15 Less taxation	*27*	*43*	*54*
16 Net profit after tax (14 − 15)	*30*	*47*	*63*
17 Dividends	*20*	*25*	*25*
18 Retentions	*10*	*22*	*38*
19 Cash flow	*26*	*37*	*63*

Notes

Figure 4:3 Analysis of X Engineering Ltd

PART 2 BALANCE SHEET ANALYSIS (£,000)

Position as at	31-12-70	31-12-71	31-12-72
Fixed assets			
20 Land and buildings (net)	141	128	155
21 Plant and equipment (net)	25	20	28
22 Others (net)			
23 Total fixed assets	166	148	183
Miscellaneous assets			
24 Investments (unquoted)			
25 Investments/loans to associates			
26			
27			
28 Total miscellaneous assets			
Current assets			
29 Cash	7	20	4
30 Investments (quoted)			
31 Trade debtors	112	134	215
32 Other debtors			
33 Stock and work-in-progress	220	260	350
34			
35			
36 Total current assets	339	414	569
37 Total assets (excluding intangibles)	505	562	752
Current liabilities			
38 Due to banks (secured)	74	45	75
39 Due to banks (unsecured)			
40 Bills payable			

41 Trade creditors	139	174	204
42 Other creditors			
43 HP commitments			
44 Current tax	5	10	50
45 Dividend			
46 Current loans:			
47 Directors' current accounts	41	74	58
48			
49 Total current liabilities	259	303	387
Deferred liabilities			
50 Mortgages			
51 Loans (long dated)	56	47	115
52 Future tax			
53 Total deferred liabilities	56	47	115
54 Total outside liabilities	315	350	502
Shareholders' funds			
55 Issued capital	150	150	150
56 Capital reserves	30	30	30
57 P and L account	10	32	70
58 Other revenue reserves			
59 Total shareholders' funds	190	212	250
60 Less intangibles			
61 Net tangible worth	190	212	250
62 Total liabilities (excluding intangibles)	505	562	752

PART 1 FINANCIAL SUMMARY (£'000)

Company *Y Brothers Limited*
Auditors *Checkit and Cost*

Audited accounts dated	June 71	July 72	Sept 73
Position as at	31-12-70	31-12-71	31-12-72
Period (if other than 12 months)			
1 Net current assets (36 − 49)	45	28	(2)
2 Current ratio (36/49%)	112	107	100
3 Net tangible worth	120	130	110
(beginning of period)			
(a) Add/deduct retentions	10	(20)	(23)
(b) Add/deduct			
(c) Add/deduct			
4 Net tangible worth	130	110	87
(end of period)			
5			
6 Gross profit ratio (%)	12.0	10.0	6.0
7 Sales (for period)	1,540	1,505	1,290
8 Purchases			
9 Gross profit	185	150	77
10 (a) Less overhead expenses			
(b) Less depreciation	75	75	70
(c) Less directors fees	45	45	35
11 Trading profit (9 − 10)	65	30	(28)
12 Other income			
13 Other expenditure			
14 Net profit before tax	65	30	(28)
15 Less taxation	25	20	(5)
16 Net profit after tax (14 − 15)	40	10	(23)
17 Dividends	30	30	−
18 Retentions	10	(20)	(23)
19 Cash flow	85	55	47

Notes

Figure 4:4 Analysis of Y Brothers Ltd

PART 2 BALANCE SHEET ANALYSIS (£'000)

	Position as at	31-12-70	31-12-71	31-12-72
	Fixed assets			
20	Land and buildings (net)	100	96	91
21	Plant and equipment (net)	180	185	189
22	Others (net)	55	51	59
23	Total fixed assets	335	332	339
	Miscellaneous assets			
24	Investments (unquoted)			
25	Investments/loans to associates			
26				
27				
28	Total miscellaneous assets			
	Current assets			
29	Cash	2	–	1
30	Investments (quoted)			
31	Trade debtors	113	110	86
32	Other debtors			
33	Stock and work-in-progress	309	313	374
34				
35				
36	Total current assets	424	423	461
37	Total assets (excluding intangibles)	759	755	800
	Current liabilities			
38	Due to banks (secured)	–	–	170
39	Due to banks (unsecured)	130	145	–
40	Bills payable			
41	Trade creditors	199	198	210
42	Other creditors	–	–	58
43	HP commitments	20	12	–
44	Current tax	30	30	–
45	Dividend	–	10	25
46	Current loans			
47				
48				
49	Total current liabilities	379	395	463
	Deferred liabilities			
50	Mortgages			
51	Loans (long dated)	250	250	250
52	Future tax			
53	Total deferred liabilities	250	250	250
54	Total outside liabilities	629	645	713
	Shareholders' funds			
55	Issued capital	100	100	100
56	Capital reserves	25	25	25
57	P and L account	50	30	7
58	Other revenue reserves			
59	Total shareholders' funds	175	155	132
60	Less intangibles	45	45	45
61	Net tangible worth	130	110	87
62	Total liabilities (excluding intangibles)	759	755	800

c

The striking point about these figures is that not only is turnover rising but the gross margin of profit is rising still faster. An adequate proportion of the profit is being retained and as a result the net worth has risen over the three years from £190,000 to £250,000.

The overall picture is therefore quite good, although not over liquid, and the only question which needs to be asked is whether it is possible for the profit trend to go into reverse and fall over the next few years as rapidly as it has risen over the last three years. As long as a reasonably reassuring answer is given to this question the company should prove a good risk.

If it is found that the general trade standing of X Engineering is good — that is, provided that the good impressions given by these accounts are supported by the general esteem in which the directors are held — this company might be considered as good for credit up to the £35,000 level if necessary. (Almost certainly, however, company X will ask a supplier for ninety-day terms, as it will be seen that the creditors figure is high.) This extended credit should be quite safe for the supplier to grant, provided his selling price covers the cost of ninety days' credit.

This credit assessment of £35,000 is based on the following calculations:

1   It is well under 25 per cent of total creditors (£204,000 — item 41). Moreover, if turnover continues to rise this percentage will tend to fall further. (No single creditor should normally represent more than a quarter of the total unless there is a very special relationship between the two parties.)
2   £35,000 is covered handsomely by net profit (£117,000) and cash flow (£63,000).
3   With this ample cover no great concern need be felt as a result of the rather mediocre current ratio (147 per cent).

The picture painted by the next set of accounts is very different. Y Brothers Limited is an old-established family business suffering from too much competition from cheap imports. The gross profit margin has fallen over three years from 12 to 6 per cent. Net tangible worth has declined from £130,000 to £87,000, while it will be noted that the bank, formerly unsecured on the company has now taken security (a floating charge). The current ratio has declined from 112 to 100 per cent.

These figures show that company Y is in serious trouble. Unless present trends are reversed immediately the net tangible worth will shortly be a negative figure (in other words there will be a capital deficiency). There is a further disquieting factor in the stock figure for, despite a fall in turnover in the last two years from £1,540,000 to £1,290,000, stocks and work-in-progress have risen from £309,000 to £374,000, a rise of 21 per cent. This means either that the company has taken delivery of goods in anticipation of sales which have not materialized or – even worse from the creditors' point of view – the stock figure has been inflated to try to hide unsuccessful trading. In either case this increase in stocks is a red warning light to any wide-awake creditor.

If there are still any doubts about whether this is a creditworthy balance sheet they will quickly be dispelled by a calculation of the break-up value (Figure 4.5). The percentages used for this purpose are those suggested on page 41.

	Book value	Estimated to realize
Cash (100%)	1	1
Debtors (80%)	86	69
Stocks (33%)	374	125
Motors (20%)	59	12
Machinery (50%)	189	94
Leaseholds (75%)	41	31
Freeholds (100%)	50	50
Goodwill (nil)	45	Nil
	845	382

Less: Bank secured by general
charge on assets   170

     212
Less: Unsecured creditors   543

Deficit as regards
unsecured creditors   331

Issued capital   100
Deficit as regards ⎫
the members of ⎬ 431
Y Brothers Ltd ⎭

Figure 4:5 Break-up value of Y Brothers Ltd (£'000)

On this basis against unsecured creditors of £543,000 there are, after satisfying the bank, realizable assets of only £212,000 or a possible dividend of around 35p to 45p in the £. The shareholders of course stand to lose every penny of their investment.

Before leaving this example it may be of interest to see what the situation would have been had the bank not had a charge over the company's assets. On the same assumptions made above the assets would still have realized £382,000. Unsecured liabilities, however, would have totalled £713,000 including this time the bank. There would still have been a deficiency towards the unsecured creditors but they would nevertheless expect to receive a dividend of about 52p in the £. This shows how the unsecured creditor's position changes for the worse as soon as the bank secures itself on the debtor company. It is not at all unusual in practice for there to be no dividend whatsoever for unsecured creditors in a liquidation where the bank has a charge over all the assets.

Assessment of the ABC Manufacturing Company Ltd

The latest year's accounts of this company have already been examined in Chapter 3. It was seen that, although the company is making some profits, it is not very liquid and the stock forms a rather high proportion of current asets.

The analysis in Figure 4.6 shows three years' comparative figures for the company and the position becomes rather clearer.

Current position

Although the overall current position is apparently improving, this is entirely because of an increase in stock and work-in-progress which has risen by 20 per cent in three years compared with a 4 per cent increase in turnover over the same period.

If stock of £710,000 was adequate three years ago to support an annual turnover of £4,610,000, is the stock figure now too high at £850,000 in relation to turnover of only £4,798,000? There are a number of possibilities: perhaps the company was previously under-stocked or is now expecting a substantial increase in turnover (or in prices of its raw materials) and is increasing stocks accordingly. It is unlikely, although not inconceivable, that the directors have written up the value of the stock artificially because this would increase the tax charge.

Perhaps the best clue to whether the stock figure is reasonable or not is given by the number of days' sales represented by the stock held at the end of the year. On this basis stocks are now equivalent to 64 days' sales compared with 56 days' sales three years ago. At 64 days the stock figure does not seem to be excessive for a manufacturing company.

An additional problem facing the directors of the company is that the £500,000 debenture loan stock will have to be redeemed or renewed two years hence (1975) and this may pose problems. It will be seen that quoted investments have risen from nil to £110,000 over the three-year period and it may be intended to build these up to provide an easily marketable fund from which the loan can be repaid. There is no doubt, however, that, on present figures, a repayment will throw a heavy strain on the company's finances.

The current position, therefore, is not strong although in the immediate future there does not seem to be serious cause for concern.

Profits

The gross profit margin has fallen over three years from 7 to 5.8 per cent on sales, with the trading profit down over the same period from £254,000 to £205,000. This is a poor return for a manufacturing company. In the last trading year, moreover, the company derived a useful £80,000 from 'other income' compared with £25,000 net the previous year. Were it not for this increment, the overall position would be a good deal worse than it is.

An attempt should be made to assess the future level of 'other income' as if this item is to revert to the previous level, and if trading profits continue their decline, it would appear that the company is running into trouble.

Net tangible worth

At first glance the improvement in net tangible worth is quite satisfactory having risen from £604,000 to £825,000 over the last three years. However, this improvement reflects the £80,000 'other income' for 1972-3 together with the increase in stock and it cannot therefore be assumed that this rising trend will continue. Much depends on the future level of 'other income' and general profitability of the company – that is, whether the increase in stock foreshadows an increase in turnover and trading profits.

PART 1 FINANCIAL SUMMARY (£'000)

Company *ABC Manufacturing Company Limited*
Auditors *Tickit and Vouch*

Audited accounts dated	June 71	July 72	July 73
Position as at	31-3-71	31-3-72	31-3-73
Period (if other than 12 months)			
1 Net current assets (36 − 49)	319	400	509
2 Current ratio (36/49%)	140	149	158
3 Net tangible worth (beginning of period)	494	604	700
(a) Add/deduct retentions	110	96	125
(b) Add/deduct			
(c) Add/deduct			
4 Net tangible worth (end of period)	604	700	825
5			
6 Gross profit ratio (%)	7.0	6.5	5.8
7 Sales (for period)	4610	4650	4798
8 Purchases			
9 Gross profit	325	300	278
10 (a) Less overhead expenses			
(b) Less depreciation	18	20	20
(c) Less directors' fees	15	15	15
11 Trading profit (9 − 10)	254	227	205
12 Other income	35	35	80
13 Other expenditure	15	10	
14 Net profit before tax	274	252	285
15 Less taxation	109	101	105
16 Net profit after tax (14 − 15)	165	151	180
17 Dividends	55	55	55
18 Retentions	110	96	125
19 Cash flow	128	116	145

Notes

Figure 4:6 Analysis of ABC Manufacturing Co. Ltd

PART 2 BALANCE SHEET ANALYSIS (£'000)

	Position as at	31-3-71	31-3-72	31-3-73
	Fixed assets			
20	Land and buildings (net)	460	470	475
21	Plant and equipment (net)	245	250	256
22	Others (net)	25	25	30
23	Total fixed assets	730	745	761
	Miscellaneous assets			
24	Investments (unquoted)	55	55	55
25	Investments/loans to associates			
26				
27				
28	Total miscellaneous assets	55	55	55
	Current assets			
29	Cash	10	6	8
30	Investments (quoted)	–	50	110
31	Trade debtors	367	405	390
32	Other debtors	30	35	30
33	Stock and work-in-progress	710	734	850
34				
35				
36	Total current assets	1117	1230	1388
37	Total assets (excluding intangibles)	1902	2030	2204
	Current liabilities			
38	Due to banks (secured)	219	237	325
39	Due to banks (unsecured)			
40	Bills payable	112	150	11
41	Trade creditors	379	349	443
42	Other creditors	15	19	25
43	HP commitments			
44	Current tax	38	40	40
45	Dividend	35	35	35
46	Current loans			
47				
48				
49	Total current liabilities	798	830	879
	Deferred liabilities			
50	Mortgages repayable 1975	500	500	500
51	Loans (long dated)			
52	Future tax			
53	Total deferred liabilities	500	500	500
54	Total outside liabilities	1298	1330	1379
	Shareholders' funds			
55	Issued capital	310	400	400
56	Capital reserves	310	355	400
57	P and L account	10	10	15
58	Other revenue reserves	274	235	310
59	Total shareholders' funds	904	1000	1125
60	Less intangibles	300	300	300
61	Net tangible worth	604	700	825
62	Total liabilities (excluding intangibles)	1902	2030	2204

With net tangible worth of £825,000 there is clearly a substantial cushion so far as unsecured creditors are concerned and again there is no immediate cause for concern although in view of the £500,000 loan stock falling due for payment in 1975 the bank is likely to obtain security before then and this will affect the position of unsecured creditors.

Break-up value

The calculation on page 45 shows that on the basis of a fairly heavy writing down of asset values the company would not quite pay 100p in the £ to creditors. It will be appreciated, however, that this calculation is very much a shot in the dark and illustrates the difficulties of assessing credit by this method.

Assessment

The picture revealed by the accounts of the ABC Manufacturing Company is of a substantial business which is rather illiquid and whose trading profits show a declining trend. The real trouble is the profit margin and if this were to improve the other problems facing the company would be largely eliminated.

There is no great problem if all that is required is £2,000 to £3,000 credit as, with the substantial net worth, such figures are no more than an average trade risk, but this company might well require £20,000 to £30,000 credit on a monthly basis from its principal suppliers. Would such figures be safe? The answer probably depends on whether the goods in question are to be supplied from stock or whether they are subject to a continuing contract with perhaps an investment in specialized plant, and so on, by the supplier. If goods are merely being supplied from stock the supplier should have no difficulty in extricating himself fairly quickly should payments become slow or the declining trend in profits continue to the point where it endangers the company's safety. If the £20,000 − 30,000 monthly credit represents a contract to supply goods over an extended period, and particularly if the supplier will have to 'tool up' specially for the contract, the risk should probably not be taken unless special payments arrangements are made.

The point to be noted is that the ABC Manufacturing Company Limited does not seem to be in danger of failing in the immediate future but the crisis is likely to come in two years' time. A credit exposure of, say, £25,000 sometime during 1968 appears to be reasonably safe but a prudent supplier involved for such an amount should take care that he is in a position to reduce his exposure if necessary. At £25,000 this is a high-risk account which should be watched very closely for any signs of deterioration.

Note on accounts analysis forms

In part 1 (financial summary) of the accounts analysis forms it will be noted that profit trading (item 11) cannot be exactly related to gross profit (item 9) because of the fact that published profit and loss accounts as a rule do not contain a great deal of information regarding overheads (item 10a). This will be appreciated if the profit and loss account of the ABC Manufacturing Company, shown in Figure 3.1, is compared with the financial summary in Figure 4.6. Working purely from the profit and loss account, overhead expenses might be thought to amount to no more than debenture interest (£35,000) and auditor's remuneration (£3,000). In fact overheads cover the whole field of administrative and selling expenses as well as interest costs. Overhead expenses (item 10a) are therefore left blank in these examples, as this information is not usually available in practice.

CHAPTER 5

Terms of Sale

'The longer the terms, the greater the risk' and 'the longer the terms, the greater the cost' are two maxims relevant to this chapter.

In terms of risk and cost alone, one should give as little credit as possible. However, the ability to give credit itself creates sales opportunities which would not be there without it. For instance, a man may have a flair for selling but have very little capital. He may be capable of establishing a successful shop but, having no capital, he cannot pay his suppliers until he has sold his wares and received payment from his customers. His suppliers must therefore either give him credit or forgo the opportunity to trade with such a man.

Having established whether it is prudent to give credit to a new customer (by making the inquiries referred to in Chapter 2 and coming to a decision on that point), the question of how long he is given to pay must be examined. In many trades there are recognized and established trade terms and, within those trades, there are also recognized alternatives and exceptions. In other trades there may be different terms and in some there may by no established pattern, it being a matter for negotiation between buyer and seller.

In terms of sheer time saving it is preferable, other considerations being equal, to extend the amount of credit, in terms of *time*, consistent with the normal trade practice and moreover to give the same settlement discount. Most people in a given trade are familiar with the established terms and to adhere to general practice avoids misunderstanding, delays, correspondence, and, ultimately, additional risk.

Monthly credit

The majority of trade credit granted in the UK is on monthly terms. This, however, does not necessarily mean payment will be made or is even meant to be made in 30 or 31 days from despatch or receipt of goods. Most commonly it means payment on or before the last day of the month following the date of the invoice.

If the same value of goods is despatched each day in March the invoices would all, on these terms, be payable on 30 April. The average despatch date in March would be the sixteenth and therefore the actual period of credit granted would be 45 days.

In the dress trade settlement is due on the tenth of the month following for all despatches up to the nineteenth of the previous month. The mid-point between 20 March and 19 April is 4 April. Due date is 10 May. So in this trade monthly terms involve an average of 36 days' credit. Monthly credit in the dress trade is therefore officially 20 per cent shorter than monthly credit in many other trades.

However, in the carpet trade it is normal for payments to be due on the twentieth of the month following for all invoices issued in the previous month. This amounts to 35 or 36 days' credit, in effect the same as the dress trade although calculated from a different point.

Thus in the carpet and dress trades if every customer paid on time the debts would turn over ten times in each year, whereas on the ordinary monthly terms which involve 45 days' credit they turn only eight times a year. From this it follows that, to finance the same volume of turnover, 25 per cent more capital is needed to finance debtors on normal monthly terms than is needed in either the dress or carpet trades. For this reason alone it is important to realize what giving even normal credit involves in terms of cost of borrowing.

Quite apart from the question of financing monthly trade credit, what effect does this situation have on the total credit exposure? If sales to a customer are running at £500 a month he will frequently be in the position of owing £1,000 without being overdue because goods invoiced in one month are not due for payment by the time further goods are being despatched during the following month. If payment does not arrive on due date, and goods continue to be despatched in the third month, the amount owing can easily rise to £1,500 and so on. If the message does not pass to the despatch controller promptly, the supplier can very easily find himself in the situation where he is owed £2,000 on monthly terms by someone he rated at £500 and this is not a happy situation for either the supplier or his customer. Therefore, if a supplier wishes to sell £500 of goods each month to a customer on monthly terms then he must first satisfy himself that the customer is a good risk for at least £1,000 and preferably for £1,500 or £2,000. This may be expressed by the following formula:

credit limit should be greater than sales x terms

If this cannot be achieved then the terms must be shortened or an unwarranted risk must be taken, or the business forgone. There are no other choices.

Extended credit

'I want longer credit,' says the valued customer. 'How much will you buy?' asks the supplier. 'The more credit I receive the more will I buy,' says valued customer. If this conversation is extended to the ultimate in absurdity the supplier will sell an infinite quantity of goods and never be paid. A sale is not complete until payment is made. Moreover, no realized profit accrues until then. The supplier wishes, or should wish, to maximize sales consistent with the credit risk. If he assesses his customer as good for £10,000 then he should begin by trying to sell him £10,000 worth of goods on seven-day terms, but £5,000 on monthly terms would also be a sound arrangement. If such a customer wishes to buy £2,500 a month it may be very good business to grant three months' credit provided always the cost of the credit is built into the price of the product or forfeit in discount.

More often than not, extended credit is required by those who are in financial straits. It is vital to distinguish between two fundamentally different types of financial straits:

1   The company whose assets comfortably exceed its liabilities but whose assets are not in a sufficiently liquid form to enable it to pay accounts on time.

2   The company whose assets are exceeded by its liabilities, or which
    overvalued its assets, or which is selling stock at less than cost to
    raise quick money.

The first company may be a sound credit risk. Its customers will have
to wait for settlement and this fact will involve them inevitably in
additional interest costs and administrative overheads but it will not
involve them in the loss of the value of the goods. The second company
is heading for disaster and should not be given credit.

Owing to the extreme difficulty in evaluating unsold stocks it is, of
course, possible to overvalue this item either by mistake or deliberately.
If the stock figure is significantly inflated beyond the truth an
appearance of solvency can artificially be created in the balance sheet.
For this reason it is sometimes difficult to distinguish one type of
situation from the other. Detailed knowledge of the nature of the
company's business measured against the known norm in its trade will
help to clarify this point.

One solid conclusion may be drawn from this: if a customer seeks
credit longer than the normal terms for the trade in which he is
operating the supplier must look most carefully into the financial
situation of the customer with a view to ensuring that there is every
reasonable chance of the debt being paid on the extended due date.

Additional safeguards

Bills of exchange

It is said that a bill of exchange is no better security than any other
debt such as open credit. Technically at law this is true but in practice
there are some significant differences. If an open account debt is not
paid on due date the creditor must start by writing reminder letters of
ever increasing force until he obtains settlement or engages a solicitor to
take legal action. This is time consuming and costs interest on the
money tied up in the sale, as yet unpaid for. At any time during this
correspondence the debtor may dispute his liability to pay on some
technical ground and, if he sets his mind to his task, he can effectively
delay settlement for many months and even years. The bill differs from
this in two material respects: first, it is an unconditional promise to
pay – if there is a genuine dispute the legal burden of proof lies with

the debtor and not with the creditor; second, the bill is payable on a fixed and predetermined date and if it is not met on that date it can be sued upon without further ado, after giving the drawer and any endorsers notice of dishonour.

Arising from this there are many traders who have little compunction about postponing settlement of open accounts due but who would shrink from dishonouring a bill, which, quite apart from any other consideration, may well come to the notice of their own banker.

For these reasons bills of exchange are nearly always met on due date, unless the drawee is actually insolvent, whereas open account transactions are frequently not settled until several reminders have been issued. Bill transactions are, for these practical reasons, a better credit risk than open account transactions. Moreover, administration and interest costs, at the collection stage, are reduced or eliminated since the bill 'collects itself' on the appointed day.

It is, of course, more trouble to arrange bill transactions in the first place and the operation is not worth while for regular normal accounts which operate satisfactorily on an open account basis. Bills should, however, be considered as a mode of settlement whenever significant sums of money come in question, coupled with extended credit (from as little as 60 days up to six months and more, but most commonly 90 days) or where there is reason to believe that settlement will be delayed still further if open account terms were agreed.

Bills were very much in fashion before the First World War but went out of fashion after the war, so far as trade within the UK was concerned. In the last ten years they have been coming back into fashion as people have become increasingly aware of the importance of receiving payment when due and the cost of failing so to do.

Endorsement of bills and guarantees

If there is still some doubt about whether an accepted bill is likely to be met by a debtor company, additional security can be obtained by arranging for another party to endorse the bill – this is done by the other party just signing on the back. There is naturally resistance to such a request. However, it is not unknown for a wealthy person or concern to form a new company with only nominal capital and, if that company has occasion to seek extended or substantial trade credit, it is only prudent and reasonable to insist on some guarantee from the party backing the new venture. There is little difference in effect between drawing up a guarantee and endorsement on a bill. Endorsement has two marginal advantages: it is quick and easy; it is unequivocal and cannot later be called in question, which might happen to an inadequately worded guarantee. It must, however, be quite clear from the endorsement who the endorsing party is.

There is even marginal value in obtaining the endorsement of directors in their personal capacities, even if they are not wealthy. If the bill is not met, they then become personally liable for the debt — severally and jointly — and if they do not pay they may be forced into personal bankruptcy. Again there are those who would shrink from this step but who might not shrink from allowing their limited liability company to default and fail. Suspicions should be aroused if directors offer personal guarantees freely. They may have done this to many other creditors and such guarantees freely offered are the more likely to be worthless. Evidence of personal worth is not easy to obtain or establish in this country without the cooperation of the guarantor, and if he really is worth so much one might be forgiven for wondering why he does not trust his own business with a little more of his own capital.

Little store should be set by directors' personal guarantees and endorsements. Their main value lies in the deterrent effect that fear of bankruptcy may hold for them.

Promissory notes

Whereas a bill is commonly drawn by a creditor and is accepted by a debtor, a promissory note is drawn by the debtor. Like a bill it is an unconditional promise to pay. They are not common in UK trade practice and have no practical advantage over the more familiar bill of exchange.

Post-dated cheques

Much more common and much akin to the promissory note is the post-dated cheque. Like a bill this is also unconditional and can be sued upon without other proof of debt. Unlike bills, which are usually drawn at the outset of a transaction, the post-dated cheque is usually drawn in postponed settlement or part settlement of a debt already past due. They therefore normally reflect an unsound financial situation though there are exceptions. A post-dated cheque is better than nothing, as half a loaf is better than no bread. When it arrives the question of proof is at least past and the amount of the cheque and the extent to which it is post-dated will, in the light of later developments — that is, its being met on presentation — provide valuable information for future credit assessment.

Normally further credit should be curtailed upon receipt of a post-dated cheque. If the maturity date is too far ahead it may be wise to insist on earlier settlement but in no case should such a cheque be returned to the drawer until he has met his liability.

Short credit

A common problem arises where, if monthly credit is extended, a supplier may be faced with the choice of granting too much credit in terms of value or forgoing the business. For example, half a grand piano cannot be sold to anyone; if the prospective customer is not a good risk for the full value of the piano some practical solution, which is also acceptable to the customer, must be found.

Pro forma

A pro forma invoice requires payment before despatch of goods. This involves no credit risk whatsoever. Its most frequent use is between traders who are unknown to one another and where the buyer is unable to provide satisfactory trade references or is in a great hurry.

Cash on advice of availability

Similar in effect to pro forma, this is more commonly used where orders are placed before manufacture. The supplier advises his customer when the goods are ready and payment is then due before delivery.

Cash on delivery (COD)

This of course is a commonplace arrangement for sales to private individuals but it is little used between traders where open credit is arranged or, failing this, a pro forma invoice is the more usual alternative.

Seven and fourteen days (open credit)

There is little difference in principle between these terms and any other open account terms (see the section on monthly credit on page 61). In certain trades seven-day terms are the normal basis of business and when this is so it is generally unwise to offer longer terms. In some trades it is common to offer alternative terms with variable settlement or cash discounts, for example, monthly terms with 2½ per cent settlement discount *or* seven-day terms with 3¾ per cent settlement discount. Again some suppliers will give a 5 per cent or even 6 per cent discount for settlement within seven days.

The cost of giving such large discounts for prompt settlement must be carefully measured against the overall profit and risk in the transaction. It is useful to use short terms where a large turnover is anticipated with customers of strictly limited credit standing. It is also sensible where perishable goods are involved or where the next sale down the line is for cash. It would for instance be both unnecessary and imprudent to grant monthly credit for raw animal skins or fresh strawberries. Longer credit is more feasible when business is transacted in pickled skins or frozen foods. As a general principle short credit is normal at the primary producing end of trade with terms lengthening as the chain of production grows and likewise discounts tend to be larger with finished goods than with raw materials.

However, even with finished goods it should be appreciated that by insisting on seven-day terms instead of monthly terms much greater turnover can be achieved with less credit risk. If a customer is good for no more than £500 credit at any one moment he can buy only £3,000 a year on monthly terms but on weekly terms he can buy around £25,000 of goods a year without exceeding the figure of £500 at any one time.

Load over load

This term of sale is an effective self-operating form of credit management but its application is limited to certain trades and many people are unfamiliar with it. It is for instance commonplace in the petrol trade between the large oil companies and their customers the garages. At any one moment the garage has credit for one supply of petrol. When the tanker next calls to refill the pumps, payment is due and furthermore it is made, otherwise the pumps are not filled. This arrangement avoids financial trouble for both supplier and customer and could be practised more widely in many trades where regular replacements of goods are required.

Fifty per cent cash fifty per cent credit

This may be termed a compromise solution to a credit problem with a new customer. It takes some of the pain out of pro forma invoice or COD terms but, from a security angle, it is much superior to open account terms. If the customer can produce cash or a current cheque for half the value of his requirements, it is not unreasonable to take a chance on his being able to produce an equal sum on a later occasion, especially when he has on-sold at a profit. Thus the total credit risk is halved from the outset and, in effect, half the sale has been completed even as to payment.

This arrangement, although not particularly common, does have an appeal to people's sense of fair play as each party participates in some risk – the buyer is risking being unable to sell the goods for which he has already paid and the seller is trusting the buyer with half of his goods. Thus a sense of mutual trust is established at an early stage in the relationship and, curiously enough, most people respond to this type of situation. Moreover, it has little appeal to the rogue who has no intention of paying from the outset. He is more likely to seek out a less careful supplier whom he can take for a complete ride instead of only half a ride. Half a ride is in fact not much use to the rogue as his plan is to obtain free credit and sell for cash under cost, and quickly. Since he is not going to pay anyway the fact that he sells under invoice price is irrelevant to him. This arrangement therefore not only has the various risk-reducing benefits outlined but also tends to weed out the rogues.

Working to a preset credit limit

This is often a more satisfactory solution to a credit problem than at first appears likely. Many would-be credit givers shrink from the prospect of discussing anything so delicate as a credit rating with the person who is being rated. They feel it is rather like going up to a person and saying: 'I don't altogether trust you.'

Certainly this approach is difficult from a cold start. However, it not infrequently happens that a hard-working distributor or wholesaler really does succeed in promoting the sales of a product on credit. As he has to give credit, he also needs credit from his supplier. It may also be that sales are somewhat erratic rather than consistent. A solution to such a problem is to agree both a time limit and an amount limit from the outset. For example, the supplier may grant 60 days' credit with a £3,000 limit. If the £3,000 limit is reached after 50 days and further supplies are required the customer pays a cheque to reduce the account (although not yet due) in order to obtain further supplies without exceeding the preset credit figure of £3,000. This arrangement works very well between two honest businessmen: the buyer appreciates receiving a predetermined amount of trust expressed in money terms; he appreciates the fact that he cannot reasonably want more stock unless he has sold most or all of what he has already bought; the opportunity to restock is obviously worth having because this creates a further profit opportunity; the supplier at the same time can increase his sales and hence his profit while running a limited and predetermined risk rather than an open-ended risk potentially unlimited.

This technique is appropriate when dealing with small businesses whose outlook is progressive but whose resources are limited. It is unnecessary with firms possessing substantial resources and is probably not workable with larger organizations where these aspects of business are delegated to a level at which judgement is not exercised. Conversely, when two intelligent people are trading with one another it is a way whereby mutual trust can be quickly established and revisions can be made in the light of trading experience, if for no other reason than that a possible source of embarrassment has been faced squarely from the outset and mutual agreement has been reached.

Contra accounts

This subject is a cause of confusion and trouble to many accounts departments and it can lead to serious loss situations where one party goes or is put into liquidation or bankruptcy. A few words on the subject may therefore be appropriate.

Here we are considering the customer who supplies his supplier. He therefore appears both in the bought ledger and the sales ledger. Many firms are, frankly, sloppy in handling this situation: 'We don't need to worry about Fred, we owe him as much as (or more than) he owes us.' What really is the position on contra accounts? This depends on how they are conducted. If they are habitually offset then a right of set-off may be established by conduct. If the customer goes into liquidation owing £200 to the supplier and the supplier owes his customer £200 for purchases, the supplier may seek to claim a right of set-off. The position is quite different if cheques are exchanged. If each settles his debts when due no right of set-off obtains.

The moral of this may at first sight appear to be: 'never pay a contra account.' Such a philosophy will lead quickly to mutual distrust. The argument starts: 'I won't pay you, if you won't pay me.' Then somebody pays. If the liquidation of one party comes about, another argument arises, which may have to be taken to court. This is an expensive procedure and the conclusion is far from foregone. The court will endeavour to establish whether or not a right of set-off exists, based on the previous conduct of the two accounts. More often than not, this previous conduct will have been inconsistent and, for this reason alone, the judgement may go either way. In such a confused situation it is unlikely that costs would be awarded to the winner. All parties lose.

Special care should therefore be taken with any contra account and, irrespective of the amount a supplier may owe the customer, he should not grant him more credit than he considers it prudent to do on this consideration alone. If he conducts his affairs in such a tidy way he is unlikely to find himself in court, but if by some mischance he does the judgement will be quick and clear because the facts of conduct are clear.

Whichever way these arrangements are conducted it is both prudent and helpful to have an exchange of letters between the parties, setting out the intentions of the parties as to settlement. Provided those intentions are subsequently implemented in practice, legal difficulties in the event of a failure or even an argument will be minimized.

Contra bills

It has been known for parties owing each other money to exchange bills. This is a most dangerous practice. If a supplier draws bills on a customer and then endorses them before discounting them with a banker, he, the supplier, incurs a liability to the banker if the customer fails to meet the bills. If at the same time the customer draws bills on the supplier which he accepts the supplier is liable on those bills too. Therefore, if the customer fails, far from having any right of set-off the supplier is liable on all the bills — both his own and his customer's. This type of arrangement can bring about a chain-reaction of downfall — yet the parties can be blissfully unaware of this trap. Bills of exchange and contra accounts do not mix — they spell disaster.

To conclude the whole question of contra, such accounts should be settled regularly by payment. Failing this, they should be checked and offset at regular intervals. In either case the mode of settlement should be agreed in writing between the parties and, moreover, adhered to. If these precautions are neglected then a nasty surprise may be in store for someone.

CHAPTER 6

Assessment and Control of Credit Accounts

If credit management is to be effective it is vital to assess each credit risk, however approximate the initial assessment may be. Without an initial assessment there is no base from which to exercise effective control of an account and situations will tend to deteriorate, possibly very gradually — indeed almost imperceptibly. If balances increase gradually they may well go unnoticed by anyone, for it is a natural human tendency to say: 'Well, we are already owed £500 so another £50 is neither here nor there.' If this thought process is repeated for a number of months, what happened to begin as a reasonable credit risk may well grows into a serious problem embarrassing to both the supplier and the customer.

When as much credit information as is sufficient to make a reasonable credit judgement has been obtained, the credit assessment amount should be recorded on each customer's record or ledger card. It is equally important to revise this assessment figure in the light of subsequent first-hand experience because first-hand experience is generally a more reliable guide than any amount of opinions from third parties.

Assessment of new accounts

When opening a new account, it is impossible to do better than make a reasonable guess at an assessment figure. This is done by weighing the information obtained from representatives, from trade references, from credit inquiry bureaux, from bank reports and, if they are obtainable, from the customer's balance sheet and accounts. Perhaps the most important feature of information is whether or not it is up to date; little reliance can be placed on stale information.

The initial assessment figure should not exceed that spoken for by a trade referee, unless there is other better information. It should not be based on figures mentioned in unsatisfactory trade references or bank reports. If possible it should be within a credit bureau rating and it should not be more than twice that rating unless there is other reliable information which indicates the rating is wrong. It should also not exceed the customer's reasonable initial requirements. This last point is often overlooked but in fact it pays no one to overstock a customer; if sales go surprisingly well, deliveries can be increased and any credit assessment can be reviewed upwards to cater for the unexpectedly good trade. Therefore, the starter figure will tend to be a rather conservative figure whenever possible. At the same time, the *credit terms* must be noted on the customer's card as it will be impossible to measure the payments performance against the original assessment if these terms are not both known and recorded. The terms also have to be recorded if a successful collection procedure is to be instituted which is neither too quick nor too slow. (See also Chapter 7.)

Assessment of old accounts

Even when all precautions have been taken and properly recorded the subsequent performance may show discrepancies either way: one customer may turn out to be a slow payer who has been overassessed, another will pay promptly and order more supplies. The starter figure or initial assessment should therefore be reviewed as soon as there is sufficient payment performance to gauge. A crude but useful rule of thumb here is to assess credit at twice the highest payment made on time and free of any duress. This applies particularly to accounts with monthly credit terms.

			Terms:	Monthly
			Rating:	£500
			Assessment:	£750

Invoice Date	Due Date	Item	Debit	Credit	Balance
3-3-72	30-4-72	10 Recorders	£350		£350
7-4-72	31-5-72	9 Recorders	£315		£665
28-4-72	31-5-72	3 Recorders	£105		£770
1-5-72		Cheque		£350	£420
15-5-72	30-6-72	8 Recorders	£280		£700
1-6-72		Cheque		£420	£280
9-6-72		Credit note		£140	£140
12-6-72	31-7-72	10 Recorders	£350		£490
26-6-72	31-7-72	4 Recorders	£140		£630
30-6-72		Cheque		£140	£490
1-7-72	31-8-72	10 Recorders	£350		£840
1-8-72				£490	£350
10-8-72	30-9-72	6 Recorders	£210		£560
31-8-72		Cheque		£350	£210
11-9-72	31-10-72	12 Recorders	£420		£630
2-10-72		Cheque		£210	£420
16-10-72	30-11-72	15 Recorders	£525		£945
1-11-72		Cheque		£420	£525
13-11-72	31-12-72	13 Recorders	£455		£980
1-12-72		Cheque		£490	£490
5-12-72		Credit Note		£35	£455

Figure 6:1   Sales ledger account of Sound Traders Ltd in the books of I. M. Careful Ltd

Figure 6:1 illustrates a well-conducted moderate-size account. The two trade references both reported prompt payments: one spoke for £400 and the other spoke for £800. The supplier's representative, who is both experienced and intelligent, estimated sales might go at the rate of between six and twelve items a month at an average price of £35. The inquiry bureau gave a rating of £500 and stated that, although the issued capital of the company was only £500, the directors were experienced in the trade and had been established for over five years during which time there had been no adverse reports. Traders, they said, expressed satisfaction with the account which, incidentally, was situated in a good trading location.

In the light of all this information the supplier's credit manager made an initial assessment of £750 and noted the terms on the card. He told the book-keeper to do two things:

1 To show him the account as soon as the balance exceeded £750 – the 'amount bell'.
2 To show him the account as soon as it was three days overdue – the 'time bell'.

Accordingly, he was shown the card on 14 July when the balance had risen to £840 (from £490). Up to that point the account had not been overdue and so there was no occasion to examine it earlier. He asked himself two questions:

1 Is the account overdue?
2 Is the balance dangerously high in the light of performance to date?

The answer to both questions was no and he increased the assessment figure to £850. The card was again shown to him on 16 October at £945 and the same questions were asked. In the light of the prompt payment on 1 August, the credit manager had no hesitation in increasing his assessment to £1,000. The credit management of such an account presents few problems – it is easier to say yes than no and, in this particular case, there is no reason to decline business.

However, not all accounts are so satisfactory as the example in Figure 6:2 will indicate. Here the representative again reported favourably but the inquiry bureau was not so enthusiastic. They said that the issued capital was £1,000 but capital was fully employed and payments experience was varied: although one trader reported prompt payments of £800 another said payments were a month late and he kept credit down to £300. In order to meet the trading requirements the supplier's credit manager again selected £750 as his starting figure and the account was shown to him again on 2 June when it was just overdue (the time bell rang). The credit manager thought that this had gone far enough and placed a temporary stop on further deliveries by informing the despatch manager.

The amount due at the end of June was paid in full on 12 July and the credit manager authorized the despatch of another consignment although the first signs of financial strain were just beginning almost imperceptibly to appear. Then on 15 August, after a routine reminder only £200 of the £300 due on 31 July was received. That was an 'on-account payment' fifteen days late. The customer was telephoned and

				Terms:	60 days net
				Rating:	refer
				Assessment:	£750

Part 1

Invoice Date	Due Date	Item	Debit	Credit	Balance
10-3-72	31-5-72	Goods	£250		£250
10-4-72	30-6-72	Goods	£200		£450
10-5-72	31-7-72	Goods	£300		£750
8-6-72		Cheque		£250	£500
9-6-72	31-8-72	Goods	£300		£800
12-7-72		Cheque		£200	£600
14-7-72	30-9-72	Goods	£250		£850
15-8-72		Cheque		£200	£650
16-8-72	31-10-72	Goods	£250		£900
31-8-72		Cheque		£150	£750
11-9-72	30-11-72	Goods	£250		£1,000
20-9-72		Cheque		£100	£900
30-9-72		Cheque		£100	£800
10-11-72		Cheque		£50	£750

Part 2

Invoice Date	Due Date	Item	Debit	Credit	Balance
13-11-72		Cheque		£150	£600
14-11-72	31-1-72	Goods	£100		£700
30-11-72		Cheque		£175	£525
5-12-72	28-2-73	Goods	£125		£650
10-1-73		Cheque		£150	£500
12-1-73	31-3-73	Goods	£125		£625
29-1-73		Cheque		£200	£425
1-2-73	30-4-73	Goods	£150		£575
15-2-73		Cheque		£75	£500
19-2-73	30-4-73	Goods	£50		£550
2-3-73		Cheque		£175	£375

Figure 6:2 Sales ledger account of Watchet & Windup Ltd in the books of I. M. Careful Ltd

said that some of the goods were faulty and he would be returning £100 worth of them. The credit manager took a chance and allowed another consignment to go. By this time the account was being constantly referred to him and the balance had increased to £900.

A further on-account payment of £150 was received on 31 August bringing the balance back to £750: this paid off the arrears but only £50 of the £300 then due. Meanwhile nothing more was heard about the faulty goods which were not returned. The credit manager noticed the declining size of the payments and he noticed that greater amounts were outstanding for increasing lengths of time. The sales manager, however, took a different view and after a heated discussion another consignment was despatched without the credit manager's approval. This took the balance up to £1,000.

Reminder letters were despatched which produced one current cheque for £100 and one post-dated ten days later for another £100. Frequent telephone calls produced another £50 on 10 November. At this date the account is clearly in serious trouble. The customer has probably sold the goods and used the cash to pay some other pressing creditor. It is time for remedial measures. The choice really lies between trying to keep the customer going by strictly controlled deliveries related to payments performance which would have to be discussed and agreed with the customer, or by taking swift legal action. This choice will be determined by a number of factors. It is a long, tedious, and time-consuming business nursing a poor account back to health and it may also be a forlorn operation if other creditors choose to take advantage of this by applying legal pressure to extricate themselves. However, if there is no hope of recovering anything except by nursing the account this course may be the lesser of two evils. Before embarking on such an operation the effective cooperation and goodwill of the customer must be reasonably assured, for without this it cannot hope to work. If however, he is genuinely anxious to continue to sell the supplier's particular product it may work.

Part 2 of Figure 6:2 shows how this might be made to work and it illustrates the time and effort required on both sides. The account was in a bad state in September 1972 and effective action was taken in early November. By 2 March 1973 the account was still £175 overdue but it had been brought back under control by making limited deliveries so that the customer could continue to sell and make some profit out of which to pay off part of the arrears. It would, however, be unwise to revert to normal trading until the account is right up to date, which might take another two months.

In this example the customer has in effect been turned into his own credit controller, in that the size of the payments he has made has controlled the volume of the deliveries to him. This operation obviously cannot work if the customer does not wish to buy further supplies. If, therefore, there is no prospect of continuity, or if the customer is too far down to climb up again, it would have been better to seek a legal remedy back in early November.

Invoice date	Item	Debit	Credit	Balance
10-3-72	Goods	£250		£250
10-4-72	Goods	£200		£450
10-5-72	Goods	£300		£750
8-6-72	Cheque		£250	£500
9-6-72	Goods	£300		£800
10-7-72	Goods	£250		£1,050
12-7-72	Cheque		£200	£850
10-8-72	Goods	£250		£1,100
15-8-72	Cheque		£150	£950
11-9-72	Goods	£250		£1,200
15-9-72	Cheque		£150	£1,050
10-10-72	Goods	£250		£1,300
16-10-72	Cheque		£100	£1,200
10-11-72	Goods	£250		£1,450
11-12-72	Goods	£250		£1,700

Figure 6:3 Sales ledger account of Watchet & Windup Ltd in the books of Careless, Sellar & Co. Ltd

The example shown in Figure 6:3 shows exactly the same account being operated without credit management, whereby orders are supplied as requested and routine collection letters are sent for overdue amounts. Although nothing excessive has been ordered or supplied, payments have gradually become slower and smaller with the result that, when no payment at all arrived in November, £1,450 was owed and the normal December delivery increased the debt to £1,700. At this point both the supplier and his customer are probably in serious trouble largely through carelessness and incompetence. Yet how many firms have even a few accounts which look exactly like this one?

If Watchet and Windup Limited decided to call a meeting of creditors on 8 January 1973 because they were unable to pay the corporation tax due to the revenue man, a brief examination of Figures 6:2 and 6:3 will reveal that I. M. Careful Limited stand to lose £650 while Careless, Sellar and Company stand to lose £1,700. Yet both were receiving exactly the same volume of orders – approximately £250 a month.

In the next example (Figure 6:4) I. M. Careful's sales representative obtained an order worth £210 from S. Low and Company in the industrial town of Lichester. He estimated that the firm could handle a turnover of about £250 a month from Careful. The credit manager obtained a report on S. Low which told him that it was not a limited

			Terms:	30 days 2½%	
			Rating:	£500	
			Assessment:	£750	

Invoice date	Due date	Item	Debit	Credit	Balance
10-3-72	30-4-72	Goods	£210		
7-4-72	31-5-72	Goods	£175		£385
28-4-72	31-5-72	Goods	£195		£580
25-5-72		Cheque		£210	£370
26-5-72	30-6-72	Goods	£230		£600
19-6-72	31-7-72	Goods	£150		£750
28-6-72		Cheque		£370	£380
2-7-72	31-8-72	Goods	£270		£650
23-7-72	31-8-72	Goods	£85		£735
29-7-72		Cheque		£230	£505
5-8-72	30-9-72	Goods	£245		£750
28-8-72		Cheque		£150	£600

Figure 6:4 Sales ledger account of S. Low & Co. in the books of I. M. Careful Ltd

company. The firm had been formed in 1920 by Septimus Low whose son had taken over the running of the business in 1954. Payments were inclined to be slow but no serious complaints had been heard and the proprietor was both experienced and respected in the trade. Trade references spoke for £500 and £900, known over 'some years' and the firm was rated at £500.

The credit manager had no hesitation in approving the initial order and he assessed credit at £500 initially. Orders and repeats were then executed. The card was shown to him on 28 April because it had rung the 'amount bell' by rising to £580. Having no first-hand experience to go on, the credit manager thought this was enough to be going on with and placed a temporary stop on further deliveries until payment of the first transaction arrived. It was, however, rather too early to start pressing for payment.

On 25 May, £210 duly arrived with a new order which was executed the following day. Payment was nearly one month late but no discount was taken. The temporary stop was removed but the credit manager arranged for all orders over £200 to be referred to him. On 19 June the card was again referred with a balance of £750 and again was temporarily stopped. Ten days later a cheque arrived for £370 – again payment in full but almost one month late.

A payments pattern was by this time beginning to emerge and was confirmed in the following two months, as can be seen from the ledger record. S. Low was shorter of funds than he would like to be and just helped himself to an extra month's credit. However, he always paid in full and did not attempt to run his luck further than this. In terms of sheer economics it would have been much cheaper for him to borrow from the bank and pay his creditors a month sooner for the 2½ per cent cash discount offered. He was in effect forfeiting 2½ per cent for the privilege of postponing payment for one month. This is equivalent to paying 30 per cent a year for money. Perhaps he did not understand this or perhaps he just could not convince his bank manager that he could make effective use of additional facilities.

However, all these considerations were more for the debtor than for the supplier whose credit manager had now decided that this account, although a bit slow, was both sound and straight and warranted a limited increase in the assessment to £750. This type of account is a common feature of most sales ledgers. It represents a sound outlet for trade and therefore needs to be handled carefully with tact and discretion. Early reminders and forceful approaches may create ill-will and resentment because the customer is in fact doing his best and it is not a bad best. On the other hand it would be a mistake to regard such an account as 'gilt-edged' or 'good for any requirement'. It might most aptly be described as a second-class account worth both perseverance and watching.

Although these examples have demonstrated that credit cannot be managed by sheer rule of thumb and that tact, understanding, and discretion are an essential part of the whole technique, it can be seen from this fourth example, too, that credit equal to the highest balance or twice the highest payment not made under duress would meet the case.

Credit assessment is a guessing game, but a glance at Figure 6:4 shows that in this case a credit limit of £500 is unnecessarily tough and a credit limit of £1000 would be on the overgenerous side. This establishes the bracket within which a reasonable credit assessment figure can be fixed.

Now refer to Figure 6:5. The sales representative had met Mr Long who told him that he had to carry a wide variety of stocks which could not be turned more than four or five times a year and that, for this reason, he was not prepared to pay on monthly terms but required 90 days' credit. He already obtained this credit from other suppliers who

			Terms:		90 days net
			Rating:		£1000
			Assessment:		£2000

Invoice Date	Due Date	Item	Debit	Credit	Balance
9-3-72	9-6-72	Goods	£500		
6-4-72	6-7-72	Goods	£600		£1,100
11-5-72	11-8-72	Goods	£700		£1,800
12-6-72		Cheque		£500	£1,300
12-6-72	12-9-72	Goods	£700		£2,000
6-7-72		Cheque		£600	£1,400
9-7-72	9-10-72	Goods	£400		£1,800
8-8-72	8-11-72	Goods	£400		£2,200
13-8-72		Cheque		£700	£1,500
5-9-72	5-12-72	Goods	£500		£2,000
14-9-72		Cheque		£700	£1,300

Figure 6:5 Sales ledger account of the Long Time Co. Ltd in the books of I. M. Careful Ltd

were happy to give it. Long had built up a good trading connection and the sales representative thought this would prove a valuable outlet. He informed Careful's credit manager accordingly.

The trade references and inquiries made of the credit bureau confirmed this. Mr Long had been in this business 12 years and had gradually increased his paid-up capital from £1,000 to £9,000. The anticipated sales were about £600 a month and the credit manager, being thoroughly satisfied with the results of his inquiries, assessed the credit at £2,000 – just enough but not too much to cover reasonable requirements on ninety-day terms.

The example shows that the account is conducted impeccably and the assessment could prudently be increased in the light of this experience to a figure nearer £3,000. One of the points of this example is that the rule of thumb – twice the highest payment – must be adapted when extended credit is granted (as opposed to being taken). On a ninety-day account properly conducted, prudent credit will be equivalent to the highest balance or three to four times the highest payment made without duress.

Whenever extended credit is given it is the more important to make sure that payment is received at the proper time. Extended credit is an extra privilege which should not be abused. There is obviously a greater time lag between delivery and payment and this means there is a greater opportunity for the customer's position to deteriorate without the opportunity to detect this. The credit risk is thus not only greater in amount but greater in time. Requests for extended credit must therefore be carefully vetted and the ensuing business must be properly controlled.

Trade disputes

A dispute over the quality of goods will normally create non-payment or at least delayed payment. This in turn will make the ledger record worse in appearance. In order that he may properly interpret sales ledger information the credit manager needs to have sufficient knowledge of the trade to be able to assess disputes and how valid they are likely to be. This hazard varies from one trade to another and varies within trades according to the care a supplier takes to see his goods are correct in all respects before they leave his control.

One of the easiest ways of postponing payment is to allege fault with the delivery on grounds of quality, colour, size, price, or 'too late' or even 'too early'. If the credit manager knows that the production and despatch departments are highly efficient he is able to tackle customers confidently and effectively when faced with such allegations as excuses for non-payment. If production, checking, and despatch are inefficient he will not be able to exercise such effective control nor will he be able to distinguish so easily the valid from the invalid excuse. If he pursues a tough policy he may lose good customers, whereas, if he has to make allowances for disputes to avoid this, the less good customers may take undue advantage of the situation. This leads to longer and greater credit exposures which not only increase the risk of bad debts but also involve more working capital being tied up in debtors than would otherwise be necessary.

What are the remedies for such a situation? First the credit manager must be made aware of the production and despatch situation, whether it is on schedule, behind schedule, or ahead of schedule. He must know how quickly credit notes are dealt with, why they are issued, and what proportion of sales they represent. He must have a knowledge of the ability in the checking department and he must know what type of error is likely, unlikely, or impossible. With all this knowledge he is immediately one up on the disputatious customer, for he can call a bluff if a customer tries bluffing. If the claim sounds reasonable he can ally himself with the customer and undertake to look into the problem immediately, thereby gaining the confidence of the honest customer. He can also do this in cases of doubt.

It is vital that such problems are dealt with speedily. Drawn-out disputes undermine confidence between both parties quite apart from creating strain between the sales and credit sides of the supplier's own organization. However, in cases of doubt, the good credit manager will seek to quantify the dispute as well by asking how much of the consignment is faulty or missing. This quite often produces an answer which shows that the trouble is relatively minor even though it is annoying. In such cases he should immediately ask for payment of the undisputed part of the balance while he undertakes to the customer that his complaint will be promptly rectified. A good customer will usually respond to this type of approach and the supplier will also benefit greatly from this. It is surprising how few people bother to do this and thereby forgo the opportunity to reduce the amount owing with all the subsequent benefits which flow from this. Even if the customer declines to pay or undertakes to make a part payment but fails to do so, this all contributes further valuable information to the overall credit picture of an account.

There are some businesses which make a living out of disputes: they may or may not be financially sound but the trouble they cause by raising spurious claims and thereby deferring payment is greater in cost to the supplier than the profit on the original transaction. Such customers should be refused credit altogether and told to buy for cash or go without. Such accounts are not worth cultivating on a credit basis.

It is sometimes alleged by the clever people that to refuse to give credit is actionable at law, on the grounds that a reputation is tarnished unfairly and unreasonably by the refusal to give credit in a trade where credit is normal. This form of attack frequently succeeds: the supplier is frightened into giving credit. This is unsound. No one is obliged by law to give credit to anyone and there is no law which states 'Thou shalt give credit.' The granting of credit is a privilege and is a matter of trust.

It is perhaps actionable to state that a firm is untrustworthy but there is no need to go so far as this in refusing credit. If a credit manager feels impelled to give a reason for refusing credit — and no one is obliged to do even this — he can say quite calmly that he does not think the proposed transaction, taking everything into consideration,

D

would prove profitable. There is absolutely nothing actionable in such a statement of opinion and in this way the clever ones can be outmanoeuvred. This technique can equally well be applied to the totally uncreditworthy customer who presses for credit.

CHAPTER 7

Collection Procedure

Perhaps the most important function of all in a credit department is its collection procedure. There is no debt so bad as the one that the creditor does not attempt to collect. However excellent the credit assessment work, assessment always involves a measure of risk, guesswork and luck. Moreover, situations are bound to occur which no one could reasonably have anticipated. Efficient collection work can make bad judgments come good, just as inefficient collection work can render good judgments bad.

The fast collection of trade debts without loss of goodwill is the acid test of any credit department. In fact, the department which is efficient at collection can afford to take greater calculated risks in granting credit and still keep bad debts under control, thus benefiting sales turnover and profit.

One of the greatest causes of downfall in credit work is the temptation to defer making a firm decision. This temptation is both natural and insidious because there is always a good reason at the time for deferring action for a few days. Instead of taking 'precipitate action' the credit manager decides to make just one more telephone call to the customer to give him a last chance. The customer's secretary answers the telephone and explains that the director who signs the cheques is away at a conference for three days but will be available on Friday next. The problem is deferred till Friday. On Friday it just so happens that the director is engaged with an important customer at the moment the credit manager rings him – but he will call back as soon as he is free. He does not call back. The credit manager rings again at 4.30: line engaged; and at five o'clock: no reply. Another week has passed with nothing achieved. On Monday contact is at last made and a cheque is promised by Wednesday, but by Thursday still no cheque has arrived. This time our credit manager does get straight through to the responsible party at the other end who is profuse with apologies and explains the 'temporary difficulty'. He suggests they meet to discuss the problem but cannot possibly spare the time until the following Thursday afternoon.

In skilled hands this exercise in deferment can be carried on almost indefinitely, while a decidely weak situation deteriorates into a hopeless one. There are really only two practical alternatives in dealing with people who prevaricate or refuse to respond: either direct legal action or a short registered letter informing them that, if payment does not arrive in three days, legal action will be commenced without further intimation. Moreover, if payment does not arrive legal action must begin as promised. (See example at the end of this chapter.)

Terms and discounts

A collection policy must first be devised which is appropriate to the trade. What is required is the quickest collection procedure which the market will bear – but this will vary from one industry to another. In some trades credit is traditionally very short, and here the procedure must be very quick otherwise it will be treated as a joke. Where it is customary to give extended credit an overquick collection procedure will result in loss of goodwill and trade. However, with a unique product which is in great demand the supplier can name his own terms, whereas if his product is similar to others he must offer similar credit terms to be able to sell competitively – unless prices are substantially reduced to compensate for insisting on shorter credit terms.

Apart from credit terms, the whole question of cash or settlement discounts affects the collection procedure. Discount customs vary widely between trades and also within trades. Some trades traditionally have no discounts. Most firms will observe the discount customs of their trade because to do otherwise leads to arguments and complications unless a supplier is in a particularly strong position in relation to his competitors.

As a prerequisite to any collection procedure sales terms and settlement discounts, if any, must be clearly established and understood. For the purposes of this chapter and the examples given, we shall assume the following terms and discounts have already been established:

Normal terms. (*a*) payment in seven to ten days: 3¾ per cent discount; or (*b*) payment monthly: 2½ per cent discount.
Exceptional terms. (These do not apply unless specifically arranged in writing with individual customers.) (*a*) seven days: 5 per cent discount; (*b*) ninety days: net.

We shall also assume that the supplier is in a competitive market and there is little scope for offering price reductions as a special inducement.

Collection policy

Having considered terms and discounts, a policy can be formulated along tough lines, reasonable lines, or lenient lines. A tough policy, for instance, would involve insisting on forfeiture of discount if payment were a day late, coupled with telephoning all customers three days overdue; this, however, might be no more than a reasonable policy in a trade where the established terms were seven days' credit only. A lenient policy would involve sending monthly statements coupled with gentle reminders at monthly intervals; this may well be the right policy in certain special circumstances, but the purpose of this chapter is to concentrate on the normal rather than the exceptional situation.

There is, of course, no reason why the policy should not be varied from one customer to another: a company may choose to operate all three policies according to the degree they value the custom of their various debtors. However, if a middle policy is to be pursued for the majority of customers this can most effectively be done by establishing a routine designed to meet the majority of circumstances surrounding overdue accounts.

Collection procedure routine

The routine in this section is summarized and illustrated in Figure 7:1.

1   Statements

These will be rendered as soon as possible after the close of each month. They will normally show goods invoiced up to the end of the month which will not be due for payment until the end of the coming month.

2   Second Statement

This will be rendered one month later, a few days past due date. This statement might have a mildly worded sticker attached saying:

> May we remind you that the amount of £—— has now fallen due and your early remittance will be appreciated.

Alternatively, in cases where discount is offered, it may be considered even better psychology to send out a letter saying:

> May we draw your attention to our discount terms of 2½ per cent monthly. We shall have pleasure in allowing this discount if we receive your payment by ——day next. (Three or four days after date of writing.)

This technique will be effective in many cases because it gives a positive inducement to the customer not to delay further since he will forfeit discount if he does.

3   Mid-month reminder

If step 2 fails, the tempo should quicken a little by sending a mid-month reminder about three weeks past the due date. The tone of this letter will vary according to trade and taste but it should be brief and to the point without being curt. Its essential features are to state how much is required and exactly when it is required. To soften the effect a short sentence can be added covering the possibility of a query

Goods were despatched on 20 January and are due for payment at the end of February for 2½ per cent discount. The customer does not respond to any approach.

Date of action	Nature of action	By	To	Other action
6 February	Statement to end January	Sales ledgers	Customer	
6 March	Statement to end February and first reminder or sticker	Sales ledgers	Customer	Telephone accounts over £2,000 each week
20 March	Reminder letter (second)	Sales ledgers/Credit department	Customer	
6 April	Statement to end March via credit department	Credit department	Customer	Telephone call?
7 April	Decide appropriate action – special letter or final	Credit department	Customer	Put copy in date file for jack-up. Warn despatch/sales
15 April	Final letter Refer all transactions (if not done earlier)	Credit department Credit department	Customer Despatch/sales	
22 April	Pass account to solicitors	Credit department	Solicitors	
30 April	Transfer account to doubtful debts if still unpaid	Credit department	Company secretary/Accountant	

Figure 7:1 Collection procedure timetable

or dispute; for example:

> Would you kindly explain your grounds for withholding payment
> or let us have your remittance in settlement by return.

4   Further statement

If step 3 fails a further statement will be ready to go out shortly when
the debt is about five weeks past due. At this point it may be wise to
look into the accounts still outstanding with some care. If the
procedure has been followed on all accounts the number left reaching
this stage should not really exceed 20 per cent and more usually nearer
10 per cent of the whole ledger. Consideration should certainly be given
to advising other departments and to the possibility of curtailing, at
least temporarily, further deliveries. The credit standing should be
reviewed too and it will to some extent depend on this and the previous
history of the account what action is next most appropriate.

5   Telephone calls

If the amount is significant it is time to telephone the individual with
the power to sign a cheque – a phone call to the receptionist is usually
ineffective. Any such call should always be briefly confirmed in writing.
It is possible to introduce humour and familiarity into a telephone
conversation more easily than by writing to a firm with which there has
been no previous personal contact. It is of great long-term benefit to
establish a rapport with the bought ledger department of a large
customer or the accountant or financial director of a smaller concern.
Moreover, the telephone call may uncover some shortcoming in the
supplier's own administration such as goods not having arrived or
statements going to the wrong address. The telephone does establish
contact for certain, whereas the fate of an unanswered letter is
unknown.

   If the amount is too small to justify a phone call it may be just
worth while using one of those gaudy stickers on the statement which
can be brusque or humorous according to taste but which must be
gaudy to catch the recipient's eye.

   If the file history shows that the customer is a persistently slow
payer these further efforts at conciliatory collection are frankly just
more wasted time and expense. Even a telephone call is scarcely worth

while because we know 'the governor's out' as he always is out to all his creditors. It is better with this type of customer to bypass step 5 and move straight to step 6.

6   Final letter

If step 5 produces no result the tempo should again quicken as the situation is definitely becoming serious now. The next move should be timed ideally seven to ten days after the phone call, and certainly not more than a fortnight later. This is the 'Dear Sir, Unless . . .' stage. Again the form can vary according to taste, but the amount required must be clearly stated – there should be no need to send details which have already been sent several times previously – and payment should be formally demanded by a definite date. Furthermore, the letter should point out that failure to remit will result in the account being placed elsewhere for collection without further intimation.

There are some customers who never pay until they receive letters couched in such terms. They pay only when they see the whites of their creditors' eyes. That is why it is best to omit step 5 when dealing with such customers. The final letter is the last logical step in a credit department's routine, but it is not necessarily the end of the battle. Another uncompromising telephone call may help to convince the hardened non-payer that this credit manager really means business, but having stated the account should be placed in other hands this must be done. It is useless to bluff.

7   Subsequent actions

A policy decision must be made whether to use a firm of solicitors or a debt-collection agency or even the firm's own legal department. Preferences will vary according to experience.

Solicitors are often too busy to do justice to this type of work and are, therefore, not in a position to give collection work the attention it deserves. However, some solicitors specialize in this work and can provide a first-class service which may well work out to be cheaper than the charges of a debt-collection agency. Again, one debt-collection agency's performance and charges will vary from another's. In practice it may be best to shop around or even establish an internal legal department to take the immediate next steps. In the last resort a solicitor's services will be required to issue a writ whether or not the interim steps are handled by the legal department or the collection agency or even the solicitors themselves.

8 Doubtful debts

It is at this point that a debt should be regarded as doubtful and should be provided for. There is now nothing very useful the credit manager can do about this debt and, bearing in mind the maxim that his job is to prevent debts going bad, the further administration of the doubtful debt should be handled outside the credit area – possibly by the company secretary's department.

Some important exceptions

The routine outlined above covers all the run-of-the-mill accounts which are overdue and never reply to the credit department's approaches for payment. This routine can be delegated safely to conscientious junior staff and in any medium or large organization it should be. However, it should be realized that this routine does *not* cater for:

1 Customers enjoying special extended credit terms.
2 Customers on exceptionally short terms.
3 Customers whose balances are high.
4 Large customers.
5 Customers who reply without payment or make part payment.

These are all exceptional situations requiring special attention and treatment.

Extended credit collection

The terms must be clearly marked and it is desirable to record the due dates appropriate to each transaction so that the normal collection procedure is not instituted prematurely. This illustrates one of many reasons why the sales department must inform the credit department of special terms. When the debt eventually becomes due it will be quite possible to follow the ordinary procedure outlined above but, taking into account that the customer has already had considerable extra credit, this would be too slow and possibly also dangerous.

It can be argued that those granted special terms should be extra punctilious about adhering to them. It is therefore a good policy to telephone ninety-day accounts about fourteen days after due date and draw attention to this abuse (see page 62). There is only one satisfactory answer to persistent abuse of extended credit — revert to normal trading terms or close the account. Granting extended credit costs additional interest and, if the time is extended further, the additional cost of interest and collection work will render the whole transaction unprofitable. It follows that customers who enjoy longer terms must be more strictly controlled if they lapse from grace.

Short-term transactions

There must be a special reason why someone buys on very short terms; it might be any one of the following:

1 Special discount offered.
2 Specially low price quoted.
3 Special clearance line of goods.
4 Credit considerations.

Whatever the reason, the purpose will be defeated if the unpaid account is collected no quicker than the normal monthly account. Seven-day accounts must, therefore, be approached within ten to fourteen days of delivery and followed at weekly intervals thereafter.

High balances

As has been remarked in earlier chapters, the cost of uncontrolled credit can be enormous in terms of interest and wasted resources. To collect one debt of £10,000 will save as much interest as collecting a hundred £100 debts. Purely from the cost point of view, let alone risk considerations, large accounts require and deserve the special attention of management. They may also require an exceptional degree of tact. One useful arrangement is to institute routine reporting on large balances and according to the size of the balance it should be reported up the line. Sales ledgers, for instance, might report monthly to the credit manager on all balances in excess of £2,000 and weekly on all balances in excess of £5,000. The managing director might like to see all £5,000 accounts once a month and perhaps all £10,000 accounts once a fortnight or even every week, depending upon the amount of work involved in reporting and reading. The mere knowledge that these reports are made to 'higher authority' helps to keep staff alive to large situations, quite apart from keeping management informed, and makes it more likely that appropriate action will be taken instead of casual neglect.

Whatever the reporting arrangements underpinning the control of large balances, the routine collection procedure should be amplified so that it is very difficult for large accounts to be many weeks overdue. One practical suggestion is to arrange that all £2,000 accounts are, in addition, telephoned at step 2 of the routine procedure. This will establish polite personal contact at an early stage; if there has been some maladministration at either end this will come to light early rather than too late. These accounts should be telephoned every week if possible, and this gentle persistence will usually produce results. If, however, this does not work, even when the telephone conversation is confirmed in writing, it may be worth trying a telegram or telex message. Messages passed by these more expensive means usually receive the early attention of someone in authority at the other end and it is an effective method of extracting payment from a large company with a badly organized accounts department. If this is not effective perhaps the problem had best be referred to the financial or managing director himself. At least he cannot complain that his own staff have dragged their feet. If top management cannot devote a few moments each week to the major debtor accounts they need hardly expect their subordinates to treat their problems with the drive and attention they merit.

Again it should not be forgotten that a temporary curtailment of deliveries may work the oracle where conciliatory phone calls fall on deaf ears but this can only be employed when further orders are required.

Large customers (high credit standing)

'Large customers' in this context means highly reputable, large, nationally known companies with substantial paid-up capital. They are usually, but by no means always, public companies. They might more loosely be described as 'household names' – a useful term to describe vaguely what is meant but a horrible term to use in establishing a routine, as what is a household name to one person may not be to another.

It is with some hesitation that a supplier will press on to the writ stage when seeking payment from such companies. They know this too and, particularly in times of high interest rates and/or a tight national credit policy, some of the big battalions are not averse from stretching their payments to their less important suppliers. Many small suppliers are simply terrified of pressing their rightful claim and they meekly accept these abuses when they can ill afford to do so. This is one good reason why, as a matter of selling policy, debtors should be spread. In the situation whereby 40 per cent of sales go to one customer, that customer enjoys a position of power over his supplier and he can elect himself how quickly or slowly he pays. Credit men cannot be expected to overcome this fundamentally weak position which should in principle be avoided. However, large customers are not necessarily major customers and they may owe relatively small amounts overdue. It is not really practical politics to cut off supplies in this type of situation. Instead, the method at each collection stage is to advance one step up the customer's administrative ladder – for example, the first letter to bought ledger section, the second approach to the bought ledger manager, the third to the assistant accountant, fourth to the accountant himself, and so on. By changing the target it is possible to avoid the tenor of the correspondence becoming too acrimonious. Sooner or later someone at the other end will realize that it would be altogether less trouble just to settle this persistent applicant's account. Persistence is a virtue in such cases and may in the long term pay dividends. Someone may mark the account as one to be settled to avoid nagging.

If it is possible to make a personal call to collect the debt this can sometimes prove to be extraordinarily effective. 'My instructions are not to leave without a cheque.' This bold approach is somewhat unusual and, for this reason alone, tends to succeed because there is no established counter to such an unorthodox move.

The customer who replies without paying

There can be no set routine for this situation apart from ensuring that the credit manager sees all incoming mail affecting his area of responsibility. If this rule is followed he will see all such letters. In the light of his experience and the file records he will usually be able to judge whether the reasons given are probably true or probably a fairy tale. Whichever is the case, at least contact has been made and this should be followed up while it is still warm. Complaints should be quickly investigated. Interest should be shown in the customer's problem and an immediate request for part settlement should be made, for instance the part of the debt which is undisputed.

If there is no dispute but it is purely a question of lack of funds, the credit manager must try to gauge whether this is a temporary problem or a steadily deteriorating situation. In the first case a definite programme of progress payments should be hammered out and agreed with the customer. In the second case it may be kinder to be cruel and issue a writ as soon as possible. Harsh swift treatment will occasionally bring the customer who is drifting towards disaster to his senses before it is too late. Over-lenient creditors actually damage both their own interests and their customer's interests by encouraging him to continue in his world of make-believe — that somehow some day things will come right without any particular effort on anyone's part. It is hard work collecting from people who cannot pay but it can be even harder for them to oblige. If they are remotely anxious to co-operate effectively, they must be given every encouragement and practical assistance. Demands for settlement must be realistic in so far as it is possible to assess the customer's true capacity to pay.

If the sum at stake is sufficiently important it may be worth visiting the customer to take a first-hand look at the problem and discuss alternative courses of action. Whatever programme is thrashed out it is important that it is adhered to. It is better to have a less favourable programme which works than a more favourable programme which fails. Figure 6:2 illustrates this point.

Preparation and production of collection letters

Of necessity any series of collection letters must begin politely. Each letter in the sequence should be tougher than the one before which failed to prompt payment. The first one is usually rather mild and may even suggest that non-payment is due to an oversight. This will be effective when this reflects the true situation, as it does in many cases. It will be ineffective with the hardened slow payer who deposits all such communications in the nearest waste-paper basket. It follows that time should be saved in the production of collection letters so far as possible. This does not preclude their being drafted with great care to cover a fairly wide variety of situations. In fact, letters for all stages should be drafted so that they present a logical sequence to anyone destined to receive them all.

The less like a circular and the more like a personal letter these reminders appear to be, the more effect they are likely to have upon the recipient. It is a question of balancing the greater cost of a better production and its greater effectiveness against the cheaper but less effective circular. The decision on this point will also depend upon the volume of such letters a business requires. If less than a dozen first reminders are needed each month, there is little to be said for printing or duplicating reams of them. They might as well be typed as required. However, where there is a fair volume of both first and second reminders, the time saved by mass production will be considerable. Nineteen sample designs are shown at the end of this chapter.

Even mass-produced letters can bear the stamp of individuality if care is taken with the design of them, thus combining the virtues of effectiveness and economy. It helps if the letters are addressed specifically to the recipient and if they are personally signed. The particular amount required should always be stated.

For the benefit of those who receive such letters frequently it is desirable to have more than one version of each stage of reminder so that the changes can be rung on the customer. Letters of identical substance tend to pall after a time. For this reason there is no particular advantage in declaring to the customer which reminder he is receiving. To type 'first reminder' on a letter may be construed as an open invitation to wait for at least two more. This stricture does not apply to 'final reminder' which is helpful provided it really is a final reminder.

Subsequent reminders should also be prepared in draft form, but they should usually be specially typed as required. This is because there will be much fewer of these needed and they may have to be adapted slightly to suit particular cases. The larger the credit department the more useful it will prove to have a variety of prepared drafts for each likely occasion. These drafts can be numbered and issued in book form to all credit men and to the typists or typing pool or audio room as the case may be. This will cut down dictating time enormously: first, the credit man only has to select the appropriate letter style from the folder instead of constructing a special letter; second, he need only dictate the name and address of the customer, the amount, the letter folio number — moreover, the typist's time is also saved as she does not have to sit about listening and taking down more than the minimum details; lastly, the fact that the draft letters have been designed with care will ensure a consistently high standard of letter writing which it would not be so reasonable to expect from hard-pressed individuals dictating separate letters for each occasion.

Recorded delivery

It is useful to use this postal service whenever making a final application for payment and on such other occasions as it is considered particularly important that the customer not only receives the letter but the fact that he has received it is vouched for by an independent party. Recorded delivery is less bother to the sender than is registered post, though this should, of course, be used whenever items of value are being posted.

Other collection letters

No matter how many drafts are prepared for different situations, someone will have to write letters to deal with particular cases such as part-payment proposals or confirmation of arrangements made over the telephone. These special letters should all be scrutinized by the credit manager as it is here that the standard of correspondence can so easily slip if it is allowed to. Here are some thoughts on writing a good letter:

1   It must be absolutely correctly addressed and preferably marked for the attention of a particular person or officer in the customer's company. (This point is often not checked.)
2   It should begin both politely and crisply. If it is too curt the reader will be upset and unreceptive. If it is too woolly or cluttered with jargon the reader will be bored with its banalities.
3   It should be dignified and not obsequious in tone.
4   It should be absolutely accurate in detail of the claim. If the account is at all complicated the items should be listed and totalled on an attached sheet and should not be included in the body of the letter.
5   Ambiguity must be avoided. When writing a letter the writer will be trying to convey a message according to his own interpretation and he may not realize that his words are open to another interpreta-

tion. A checker is likely to pick up this point and this is important because in collection work the reader will naturally interpret the meaning in a way that is most favourable to himself, and this will usually be the one the writer did not intend to convey.

6   It must omit all that is irrelevant and include all that is relevant. As a general rule the whole letter should not take more than one page to cover all relevant factors.

7   Humour may be introduced when a rapport has already been established — where the writer knows his reader — but not otherwise. It may be considered impertinent or just silly by someone who does not find the situation amusing. Patronizing remarks and sarcasm should be avoided.

8   To sum up, the three virtues of a well-written letter are: *accuracy*, *brevity* and *clarity*.

Specimen collection letters

1
Use. After two routine reminders. To an important debtor or one not previously approached when discount terms do not apply for normal payment.

With statement

Dear Sirs

We enclose your statement of account giving details of an overdue balance of £———.

Would you kindly look into this and let us have your cheque in settlement or reasons for withholding your payment.

Yours faithfully,
for I. M. Careful Ltd

Credit Manager

2

Use. After two routine reminders. To an important debtor or one not previously approached when discount terms apply to normal settlement.

With statement

Dear Sirs

We enclose your statement of account giving details of an overdue balance of £—–– which is now due for payment net.

    Would you kindly look into this and let us have your cheque in settlement or reasons for withholding your payment.

Yours faithfully,
for I. M. Careful Ltd

Credit Manager

3

Use. After two routine reminders. Normal first approach by credit control when terms are net.

Dear Sirs

Despite our reminders, we are still carrying forward an overdue balance of £—–– on your account.

    May we, therefore, please have your immediate payment.

Yours faithfully,
for I. M. Careful Ltd

Credit Manager

4

Use. After two routine reminders. Normal first approach by credit control when discounts are offered for prompt payment.

Dear Sirs

Despite our reminders, we are still carrying forward an overdue balance of £—— on your account which is due net.

     May we, therefore, please have your immediate payment.

Yours faithfully,
for I. M. Careful Ltd

Credit Manager

5

Use. After two routine reminders. Alternative to 4 for debtors who have been slow before.

With statement

Dear Sirs

Despite our reminders, we still do not appear to have received settlement of your account.

     We enclose your statement and once again request your cheque for £—— by return of post.

Yours faithfully,
for I. M. Careful Ltd

Credit Manager

6

Use. As letter 5. It may be helpful to itemize outstanding invoices.

Without statement

Dear Sirs

We are surprised that despite our reminders we are still carrying forward an overdue balance of £—— on your account which relates to . . .
        Would you kindly look into this and let us have your cheque in full settlement without further delay.

Yours faithfully,
for I. M. Carefull Ltd

Credit Manager

7

Use. Where part-payment has just been received. (Polite version)

With statement

Dear Sirs

Thank you for your cheque for £—— in answer to our last letter. However, despite this payment, we are still carrying forward a balance of £—— as you will see from the attached statement.
        Would you, therefore, please let us have a further cheque to bring your account completely up to date.

Yours faithfully,
for I. M. Careful Ltd

Credit Manager

8

Use. When part-payment has just been received. (Polite version)

No statement

Dear Sirs

Thank you for your cheque for £—— in answer to our last letter. However, despite this payment, we are still carrying forward a balance of £——.

Would you, therefore, please let us have a further cheque to bring this account completely up to date.

Yours faithfully,
for I. M. Careful Ltd

Credit Manager

9

Use. Where part-payment has just been received (stronger version of 8) but account is very overdue.

Dear Sirs

We thank you for your payment of £—— in reduction of this account.

There still remains, however, a balance of £—— which is extremely overdue and we must insist on receiving your cheque in full settlement within the next seven days.

Yours faithfully,
for I. M. Careful Ltd

Credit Manager

10

Use. As 9 but for use when there is no hope of full settlement at once. To be used only when 9 will not do.

Dear Sirs

We thank you for your payment of £—— in reduction of this account.
There remains, however, a balance of £—— which is extremely overdue and we must insist on receiving a further substantial payment within the next seven days.

Yours faithfully,
for I. M. Careful Ltd

Credit Manager

11

Use. Letter to debtor enjoying 60/90/120-day terms.

Dear Sirs

We note with concern that we do not appear to have received your payment in respect of the balance of £—— on this account now overdue.
When extended terms were agreed with you, it was understood that your payments would be received strictly in accordance with these terms.
May we, therefore, please have your immediate settlement of this overdue balance or the reason for withholding it.

Yours faithfully,
for I. M. Careful Ltd

Credit Manager

12
Use. Fourth approach to large debtors only.

No statement

Dear Sirs

We are disappointed to find that no payment has been received in reply to our letter of ——.

The overdue amount is now £—— and we must insist that this receives your immediate attention.

Yours faithfully,
for I. M. Careful Ltd

Credit Manager

13
Use. Alternative to 12 suitable for smaller debtor.

No statement

Dear Sirs

We refer to our letter of —— regarding your overdue account of £—— to which we do not appear to have received a reply.

Would you kindly forward your cheque in full settlement of this account by return of post.

Yours faithfully,
for I. M. Careful Ltd

Credit Manager

14

Use. Fourth reminder for a running overdue account.

No statement

Dear Sirs

We wrote to you on ——— regarding your overdue account, but we appear to have received no reply. Further invoices have fallen due for payment making the overdue balance now £———.
  We must, therefore, insist on receiving your cheque in full settlement without further delay.

Yours faithfully,
for I. M. Careful Ltd

Credit Manager

15

Use. Fourth reminder for important accounts which one does not wish to offend – that is, instead of a 'final' and paving the way to a 'final'.

Dear Sirs

We refer to our letter of ——— regarding your overdue account of £——— and cannot trace having received your reply.
  Since we have not heard from you we must assume there is no reason for withholding payment: would you, therefore, kindly forward us your cheque without further delay.

Yours faithfully,
for I. M. Careful Ltd

Credit Manager

16

Use. Normal final application.

Recorded delivery

FINAL APPLICATION

Dear Sirs

Account £———

We note with regret that our previous applications for settlement of your now long-overdue account appear to have been ignored.

It is with reluctance that we must inform you that, unless we receive either your remittance or your explanation for not making settlement within seven days from the date of this letter, we shall be left with no alternative but to take whatever further steps we consider necessary to secure collection.

Please help us to avoid this unpleasant step.

Yours faithfully,
for I. M. Careful Ltd

Credit Manager

17

Use. Special Final. For use after normal 'final' on new accounts or accounts who received a 'final' on some previous occasion.

NOT for use on large companies.

Recorded delivery

FINAL APPLICATION

Dear Sirs

Although you have ignored our previous requests for settlement of your account, we feel sure that you would not wish us to instruct our solicitors to commence legal proceedings.

However, your failure to remit the overdue sum of £——
during the course of the next seven days will leave us with no
alternative.

In your own interests, we suggest that you settle in full the
amount outstanding before the existing debt is increased by the
addition of legal costs.

Yours faithfully,
for I. M. Careful Ltd

Credit Manager

18
Use. Final application when a part-payment has already been received.

Recorded delivery

Dear Sirs

Although we have received your remittance on —— for £——, you
will see from the enclosed statement of account that we are still
carrying forward a balance of £—— which is either due or overdue.

We very much regret, therefore, that unless we receive your
further remittance to bring this account up to date within the next
seven days, we shall be left with no other alternative but to consult our
solicitors and take whatever other steps we consider necessary to secure
collection.

Yours faithfully,
for I. M. Careful Ltd

Credit Manager

19

Use. Last resort before passing to solicitors. May be used freely on persistent late payers, otherwise only with the greatest care.

Dear Sirs

Account Due £——

Failing receipt of your cheque for £—— by return of post this account will be passed to our solicitors without further reference to yourselves.

Yours faithfully,
for I. M. Careful Ltd

Credit Manager

CHAPTER 8

Legal Action

However effective and persuasive credit management may be, there are in many trades certain customers who just do not respond to any normal approach. For them the time will eventually come when their accounts must be 'placed out of hand' or, in other words, put in the hands of another party who will try to enforce payment. Before going into the technicalities of this subject there are certain points of management principle to be discussed.

Legal action is in general to be avoided; it is expensive in both money and time. The costs of an action are never recovered in full from the debtor and the time spent in this work can usually be better employed in more constructive ways. Every account put into the hands of a third party for collection should be regarded as a failure and a mistake: a failure because almost certainly the transaction in question will by now have been unremunerative even if the debt is eventually recovered; a mistake because the initial credit assessment is now seen to have been wrong or the subsequent management of the account inadequate.

Management should, therefore, arrange to be notified on a regular basis of the number and value of those accounts put out for collection. For example, if the company prepares monthly accounts, the value of all accounts which remain unpaid, say fourteen days after they have been put in the hands of solicitors, should be provided for as 'doubtful'.

The management should not be fobbed off with the excuse: 'Oh, it's only old Charlie – he always pays when he gets the writ.' The company should not be selling to Charlie; if he survives his writ and returns for more supplies he should be told he must in future pay cash or take his business elsewhere.

In these circumstances there are two alternatives: on the one hand to employ a specialist debt collector, collection agency, or trade-protection society, on the other hand to use a firm of solicitors.

Collecting debts

Specialist debt collectors

There is a large variety of companies or firms specializing in debt collection. They range from the largest credit-reporting agencies to the very small private detective's office. In fact just about every agency discussed in Chapter 2 has a debt-collection division, as do the various trade protection societies. Some agencies specialize in general commercial work, others in the mail-order or hire-purchase fields; the specialized trade-protection societies naturally operate in their own particular trades but there are also general trade-protection societies.

Standards vary widely: the larger agencies claim with justification that they are so well established in the world of commerce that an approach by them is in many cases sufficient in itself to induce immediate settlement. This is a major advantage to their clients and it may in practice mean that a higher proportion of overdue accounts will be settled without recourse to expensive legal proceedings. At the other end of the scale it has regrettably been the case that a supplier has had as much trouble collecting from the debt-collection firm as from his actual customer. Such problems are not common, however, and certainly do not arise with the larger agencies and trade-protection societies. A modicum of care is nevertheless advisable in the choice of such a service.

Details of the various agencies' respective services are obtainable from their brochures. Charges vary; broadly speaking, the higher the cost, the better is the service. The general practice is that no charge – or only a nominal 50p or so – is payable unless at least a part of the debt is recovered. In the event of a partial or total recovery some agencies may charge their clients as much as 20 per cent – and on small sums 50 per cent of recoveries in addition to any legal charges they may have incurred, although rates as low as 2½ per cent can be obtained on sizeable debts.

The agency will normally approach the debtor by letter or telephone but in some cases they will actually call on him in an endeavour to persuade him to settle. If these approaches are not successful the agency will revert to the supplier and seek his instructions to commence legal proceedings through the agency's own solicitors. From this point onwards progress will be much the same as if the supplier's own solicitors were being used.

Agencies can be useful in other ways: they may be in a position to provide information on whether a debtor is worth pursuing – they will be able to say, for example, if he is apparently in possession of saleable assets or whether he has disappeared from his old address. Alternatively, they may know whether he is about to be made bankrupt for failing to pay a previous judgment. Such information is of value particularly when it obviates further legal costs being added to no avail.

Most agencies are prepared to undertake the tracing of debtors who have suddenly disappeared together with all their removable assets leaving only their angry creditors behind them. There is, however, no doubt that a debtor who is bent on disappearing has the advantage of his pursuing creditors.

Use of solicitors

The alternative to employing an agency is for the supplier to put the account directly into the hands of his own solicitors. The best course of action here is:

1 Employ a good solicitor.
2 *Take his advice.*

This may sound obvious but it is surprising how many businessmen with this type of problem have never sat down with their solicitors to thrash out their debt-collection policy together.

Almost every solicitor does a certain amount of this work as part of the service to his clients but, unless he has a department specializing in this work, this side of his practice is unlikely to be remunerative, involving as it does a great deal of routine paperwork and waiting about at the courts. If the supplier's business involves a fair number of accounts for collection, in other words half a dozen a month or so, he should seriously consider – again in consultation with his own solicitor – employing a firm of solicitors who specialize in this work. If his own solicitor is not well-placed to give his client an efficient service in this respect he may be able to recommend another suitable firm to handle this particular work. There is no reason why a company should not employ more than one firm of solicitors for different types of work.

Collection agencies and solicitors compared

Whether a supplier uses a collection agency or passes an account directly to his own solicitors is a matter of personal choice. Some businessmen feel that the whole question of debt collection is rather distasteful and prefer to have nothing to do with it. In certain well-defined trades there are 'closed' protection societies who handle most of the accounts for collection in that particular trade. This puts them in a strong position *vis-à-vis* the debtor who will not wish to blacken his reputation throughout the trade.

Such societies are most effective debt collectors, as are the large nationally known credit-reporting agencies who claim with justification that they are so well-established in the world of commerce that their approach is sufficient in itself to induce settlement without further recourse to legal action. Again the supplier may be carrying on business in a district where a particularly effective agency is operating. A few test cases will quickly demonstrate whether a given organization is as effective as it claims to be.

On the other hand, if the supplier has followed up his own debts properly, he may find that the only accounts which he is unable to collect himself are such 'hard cases' that the agency is unable to help without resort to legal proceedings. As the agency will certainly add its own charges to those of its solicitor and all communications between supplier and solicitor will have to be passed through the agency, it follows that it may prove cheaper and quicker for a supplier to use his own solicitors for this kind of work.

Enforcement of payment by a solicitor

This is a highly technical subject and there are many ways in which a solicitor can enforce payment of his clients' debts. What follows is a brief outline of the various courses open to a creditor to try to obtain settlement. In order to act effectively the solicitor will need to know:

1   *The exact style and address of the debtor.* It is essential that this
    information is correct otherwise not only will additional costs be
    incurred but also vital time lost in collecting the debt. It is a waste
    of time instructing the solicitor to commence proceedings against J.
    Brown and Company if the correct name of the debtor is J. Browne
    Limited. If the debtor is a firm the solicitor will have a search made
    at the Registry of Business Names to ascertain the names of the
    proprietors. If the debtor is a limited company a search will be
    made at the Companies Registry for its registered office for service
    of process to be effectively made. Inaccurate information will
    result in abortive action. The importance of correct debtor styles
    has been emphasized; it is now that the value of this care and
    accuracy becomes fully apparent.
2   *The exact details of the account to be collected.* If certain goods
    were returned by the customer for credit the credit note should be
    shown on the statement. It is easy otherwise for the debtor to
    prevaricate. Delay and expense will be the result if the solicitor
    receives a sharp reply to his letter of application and has to revert
    to his client for further information for an amended claim. It is
    therefore obvious that care at this point will be well worth while.

On receipt of the necessary information, the solicitor will write to the
debtor requesting settlement of the account within a given period of
time — generally seven days. It is unusual to commence proceedings
without first sending such a warning letter. Four things can then
happen:

1   The account may be paid (to the supplier or to the solicitor).
2   The debtor may dispute the debt.
3   He may request further time to pay.
4   He may ignore the application altogether.

If the debtor pays the matter is settled. Disputes are almost invariably
better settled out of court. If the debtor requests further time or if
there is no reaction from him the solicitor will revert to the supplier to
seek his instructions whether to commence proceedings or to agree to
further time.

Legal proceedings

Proceedings for the recovery of debts vary depending on which courts have jurisdiction over the debtor. Proceedings against a debtor resident or carrying on business in England or Wales must be started in the High Court or in a county court. In Scotland there are sheriff's courts and small debt courts (under £50). In Northern Ireland and Eire action is started in the High Court of those countries. The larger Channel Islands and the Isle of Man also have their own separate legal systems.

The remainder of this chapter is confined to describing proceedings in the English courts. The jurisdiction of the High Court is unlimited geographically throughout England and Wales. If the debt to be recovered is less than £100 the costs of the proceedings are irrecoverable. In contrast, the jurisdiction of a county court is strictly limited both geographically and as to the amount of the debt. There are nearly 450 county courts throughout England and Wales and the rules governing which of these courts has jurisdiction over a given debt depend on, for example, where the debtor resides or has his place of business, where the contract for the sale of the goods was made, or where the debt was payable. Subject to these requirements the general rule is that a county court has jurisdiction for debts up to a maximum of £750.

These are, as it were, the technical requirements governing which type of proceedings should be started. The creditor is probably more interested in the practical questions of the speed and the cost of recovering his debt and, as a general rule, it is true to say that proceedings in the High Court will bring results *more quickly* but will probably prove *more costly*.

County court action

County court proceedings will be started with the issue of a summons. In most actions for recovery of a debt a default summons will be used. Service of the summons on the defendant will usually be effected by the court and if the defendant wishes to contest the debt he must enter his defence at the court within fourteen days of service. If no defence is entered within this period, or if the defendant delivers an admission of the debt with an offer to pay the debt by instalments, the plaintiff may apply to the court for judgment to be entered, either for the whole

E

debt or in accordance with the instalment offer, and this will be done in the case of a default summons without a trial.

Alternatively, the defendant may enter a defence or admit the debt but make an offer to pay that is not acceptable. If a defence is entered a date will be fixed for a trial and judgment will be entered in accordance with the court's decision. Where an unacceptable offer has been received, a date is similarly fixed for a 'disposal' of the offer and judgment will be entered accordingly.

For certain types of debt, including those arising under hire-purchase agreements, an ordinary summons has to be used. This is served in the same way as a default summons but judgment cannot be obtained by default if the defendant fails to respond on receipt of the summons; instead the case must be heard before judgment is given and the presence of the plaintiff in court is usually required.

High Court action

Proceedings in the High Court are started by issuing a writ. This must as a rule be served personally on the defendant but, unlike a county court summons, the plaintiff must make his own arrangements for this to be done and cannot rely on the court. The usual procedure is to employ a professional process server, which, of course, adds to the expense. In the case of a limited company, however, the writ may be served by post on the company's registered office.

If the defendant wishes to defend the proceedings he must first lodge with the court a form called an appearance, and this he must do within fourteen days of service of the writ (inclusive of the day of service). Should he not enter an appearance the plaintiff may apply to the court after the fourteen days have elapsed for 'judgment in default of appearance'.

Assuming that the defendant does enter an appearance, he then theoretically has a further fourteen days to prepare and serve on the plaintiff's solicitors a copy of his defence, failing which the plaintiff may enter judgment in default of defence. In practice it is possible for the defendant's solicitors to obtain further time to prepare this defence, either by leave of the plaintiff's solicitors or, alternatively, by leave of the court. It is thus quite possible for the defendant to prevaricate for some time.

In the event of the defendant entering an appearance, the plaintiff may under certain circumstances bring things quickly to a head by applying to the court for summary judgment, otherwise known as judgement under order 14. The basis of this procedure is that the plaintiff swears an affidavit containing the details of his claim and that there is no defence. A copy of this affidavit together with a summons is then served on the defendant four clear working days before the summons is due to be heard before a master. At this hearing, if the defendant satisfies the master (usually by affidavit) that he has a prima facie defence, the master will give him leave to defend the action and he will give consequential directions about the future conduct of the proceedings. If the master is not satisfied he will allow the plaintiff to enter judgment for the amount claimed.

If the defendant has given no indication that he has grounds for disputing the claim the plaintiff is well advised to use this order 14 procedure as soon as possible because it is a speedy method of making the defendant put his defence (if any) on record. If he has no defence then judgment is quickly obtained.

Enforcement of judgment

Assuming that the plaintiff duly obtains judgment in either the High Court of a county court, he next has to decide how this judgment is to be enforced. Again there is a variety of courses open and these are described below. Which course will prove most effective will depend upon circumstances and it is sensible to confer with a solicitor when there is any doubt.

Execution against goods

Judgment can be enforced in a county court by means of a warrant of execution and in the High Court by means of a writ of *fieri-facias* under which goods belonging to the debtor can (with certain exceptions) be seized to satisfy the judgment debt.

This is a most effective method of enforcing payment provided that there are goods belonging to the debtor available to be seized. The method fails if the goods in question have been bought on hire purchase and are therefore not the property of the debtor or if they belong, for example, to the debtor's wife. Moreover, his clothing, bedding, cooking utensils, and the tools of his trade may not be seized.

These writs or warrants of execution must be satisfied in the order in which they have been issued. There may thus be a very real race between creditors to enforce their judgments on the available assets. The need for speedy action will be appreciated.

Attachment of earnings

A debt may be enforced against a judgment debtor by means of an order from a court directed to his employer to make deductions from his earnings and to send those deductions to the court so that they may go to meet the debt. Before the passing of the Administration of Justice Act 1970, a debtor could be committed to prison if he failed to obey a court order to pay by instalments. This has now been abolished except in certain cases not connected with commercial debt collection and in its place attachment of earnings has been possible since 1 August 1971 under the Attachment of Earnings Act 1971.

In theory attachment of earnings was a welcome extension to garnishee proceedings (see below) for a number of reasons: cheapness and simplicity of procedure; the possibility of making one attachment order to cover a number of debts; the desirability from the creditor's point of view of having regular, if small, payments; and the system's effect of acting as a deterrent from taking excessive credit. In practice, however, it has so far proved difficult to obtain orders. The Act specifies that the court shall order a protected earnings rate – that is to say, a sum of money which it thinks reasonable should be available to the debtor having regard to his resources and needs; it may well be, therefore, that after deduction of the protected earnings rate – and the rate is solely at the discretion of the court – there is no remainder from the debtor's earnings out of which to make any order. In addition, an order will lapse if, when made, the debtor changes employment and a fresh order has to be sought.

Garnishee order

This is a method available in both a county court and the High Court under which a judgment creditor can attach monies which are due to the judgment debtor from a third party. If the judgment creditor is aware of the existence of a debt owing by a third party to the judgment debtor, he can apply to the court for a garnishee order which requires the third party to pay over to him (the judgment creditor), out of the monies owed to the judgment debtor, the amount of the judgment debt. In case this is not clear to the reader, the following example shows how this might occur in practice:

> A Limited owes I. M. Careful £500. Careful has instituted proceedings against A Limited and has obtained judgment. Careful is aware that there are at least three other judgment creditors who are attempting to levy execution on A Limited's assets and he is worried lest the assets be insufficient to satisfy these prior claims. It then comes to his notice that A Limited are in turn owed a substantial sum by one Mr B and, after conferring with his solicitor, Careful decides to try to obtain a garnishee order on Mr B.

In this example I. M. Careful is the judgment creditor, A Limited is the judgment debtor and Mr B is the garnishee. The garnishee, Mr B, can set off any money owing to him by A Limited but not monies owing from I. M. Careful. Once the garnishee order is made it becomes enforceable on the garnishee just as if he himself were the judgment debtor.

Charging order

In the event of the debtor owning land or stocks and shares, a charging order may be obtained on these assets and a receiver appointed. This remedy is available in both the county court and the High Court but creditors are rarely in a position to avail themselves of this.

Bankruptcy proceedings and winding-up orders

Neither bankruptcy proceedings against an individual nor winding-up proceedings against a limited company are strictly methods of enforcing a judgment debt. The effects of such petitions (if successful) are to make available to the creditors as a whole the assets of the debtor so that all creditors participate equally in the insolvent estate of the debtor, subject to the prior rights of preferential and secured creditors. In practice, as every suing creditor knows, the prospect of winding-up proceedings may induce a debtor to pay.

Bankruptcy and winding-up orders are considered further in the next chapter.

CHAPTER 9

Bad Debts

Inevitably there will come a time in the best managed business when a bad debt is incurred. The aim of this chapter is to outline the circumstances in which such a loss can be suffered and the courses open to the prudent creditor to minimize and provide for his loss.

As this book is intended not only for credit managers but also for those who may be said to order the affairs of credit managers, it should be mentioned again that ideally the credit manager should not be expected to handle these matters himself. The credit manager can be likened to a doctor rather than an undertaker: his concern may, financially speaking, be with the ill or dying but is not with the dead. Such affairs fall more appropriately in the province of the company secretary who is well qualified to deal with the resulting legal problems. The credit manager should in contrast be applying himself to collecting as much cash as possible from the previous class of debtors who, although they may be ailing, are nevertheless still managing to survive.

Having said this, however, both credit managers and secretaries should know the main ways in which a company can suffer loss through bad debts.

Debtor disappears or dies

The methods available for tracing an absconding debtor were referred to in the previous chapter, but a debtor who is intent upon evading his creditors is more than likely to succeed. In many cases the debt will have to be written off completely.

It is not unknown for the estate of a deceased debtor to be insufficient to pay all his debts. The estate will be wound up by the deceased's executors or administrators as the case may be and the proceeds shared among the creditors who will thus receive a dividend on their debts of so much in the £. The winding up of the estate may prove to be a lengthy business but there is nothing that a creditor can do to expedite matters.

Bankruptcy

Bankruptcy was mentioned briefly in the previous chapter. As readers of Charles Dickens will know there was a time when insolvent debtors were thrown into a debtors' prison until such time as they were able to pay their debts. Being in prison meant that a debtor without wealthy relatives or friends had even less opportunity of paying off his creditors. The law was thus both savage and irrelevant to the problem. As a result of more enlightened ideas the principle of bankruptcy was evolved with the object of, on the one hand, sharing a debtor's property proportionally among his creditors and, on the other, allowing him to make a clean start once again.

The law relating to bankruptcy is now contained in the Bankruptcy Act 1914, the Bankruptcy (Amendment) Act 1926, and statutory Bankruptcy Rules. Before bankruptcy proceedings can start the debtor must owe a minimum of £50 to one or more creditors and he must have committed a statutory 'act of bankruptcy'. There are several classes of these acts of bankruptcy. The most important from the creditor's point of view occurs after a creditor, having obtained judgment, serves on the debtor a bankruptcy notice. If within three days of service the debtor is unable to satisfy the court that he has a valid counterclaim, or within seven days he has not paid the debt, an act of bankruptcy has been committed. Other acts of bankruptcy include:

1 Certain personal actions by the debtor to defeat or delay creditors, such as trying to evade them physically.
2 Certain dealings with property by the debtor which benefit some creditors more than others and constitute what is called a fraudulent preference.

3   The debtor's own petition against himself or his declaration that he
    is unable to pay his debts or that he intends to suspend payment of
    his debts.
4   Execution levied against the debtor's goods, where the goods are
    either sold by the sheriff or held by him for 21 days (or rather
    longer in certain circumstances).

If an act of bankruptcy has been committed by the debtor, a
bankruptcy petition may be presented to the court – either to the
Chancery Division of the High Court or to whichever county court has
jurisdiction over the debtor for bankruptcy purposes. The court will
decide whether or not to accept the petition. If it is accepted the court
makes a receiving order against the debtor.

A receiving order has the effect of vesting the debtor's assets (with
certain minor exceptions) in the Official Receiver in Bankruptcy – the
Official Receiver is in fact an office and not a person – pending
appointment of a trustee in bankruptcy. The trustee may be the
Official Receiver or a creditor or someone representing a creditor.
Within seven days of the receiving order being made (or within three
days if the debtor has petitioned against himself) the debtor is required
to submit to the Official Receiver his statement of affairs. This is
simply a list of his assets and liabilities. A public examination of the
debtor is then held at which creditors or their legal representatives may
examine the debtor regarding his past conduct and his financial affairs
generally.

Normally within fourteen days of a receiving order being advertised
the Official Receiver will call a first meeting of creditors at which it will
be decided whether to make the debtor bankrupt or alternatively to
accept a composition of his debts (see below).

If at the first meeting of creditors it is decided to make the debtor
bankrupt, the court will adjudicate him bankrupt at which point
whoever has been appointed trustee in bankruptcy will begin to realize
the debtor's assets and distribute them among his creditors according to
the Rules of Bankruptcy. If the debtor has made a fraudulent preference
the trustee may be able to obtain possession of the assets so transferred.
The subject of fraudulent preference in relation to bankruptcy and
company liquidation is treated in rather greater detail later in this
chapter.

Until a bankrupt obtains his 'discharge' he is under certain
disabilities. He may not obtain credit for more than £10 without

disclosing that he is an undischarged bankrupt. He becomes ineligible for various posts and may forfeit membership of most of his clubs and associations. He may not engage in trade on his own account or become a director of a limited company. However, his wife may employ him either directly or through a company floated especially for the purpose. If over the years he has lavished gifts on her the realization of these may help to float the new venture!

Nevertheless the disabilities of being an undischarged bankrupt are real and in due course the bankrupt may apply to the court for his discharge. Depending on circumstances this may or may not be given; or it may be given conditionally – that is, subject to the bankrupt paying a dividend of so much in the £ to all creditors. The court's general policy will be to discharge a bankrupt who has made a reasonable effort to pay back a proportion of his debts according to his means.

Creditors can in many cases expect to receive a dividend, although in most cases this will be small and in some bankruptcies there will be no dividend at all. As a general rule bad debts arising from bankruptcy should be fully written off (see page 132).

Debtor's composition or deed of arrangement

A debtor wishing to avoid bankruptcy may make a composition with his creditors – that is, arrange to pay them an agreed proportion of their debts in full and final settlement.

If a debtor subject to bankruptcy proceedings wishes to propose a composition, he must submit his proposal to the Official Receiver within four days of submitting his statement of affairs. The scheme must be approved by at least three-quarters in value and a majority in number of the creditors who have proved their debts.

Compositions can be made outside bankruptcy proceedings. If the scheme is in writing and is made for the benefit of creditors generally, the document comprising the scheme is called a deed of arrangement and has to be registered at the Board of Trade.

Why should creditors ever agree to accept a composition instead of making the debtor bankrupt? The usual reasons are:

1 A composition will avoid the *expense* of realizing the debtor's assets.

2   It will probably mean a speedy distribution instead of a considerable delay.
3   It could mean a larger payment to creditors. Perhaps the debtor has suddenly discovered, let us say, a kind-hearted uncle who is prepared to pay 35p in the £ to assist his unfortunate nephew and so save the family name. The alternative to such an offer may be a long and difficult realization of the assets. In these circumstances most bodies of creditors will settle, albeit reluctantly, for the proposed composition and the debtor will escape what some might deem his just deserts.

In a similar way a limited company may make a composition with its creditors to avoid going into liquidation, and a third party may offer to pay so much in the £ to all creditors in return for their assigning to him the full amount of their debts.

Liquidation of limited companies

Liquidations of limited companies fall broadly into two classes: voluntary liquidations and compulsory liquidations – that is, liquidations by the court. Voluntary liquidations also can be divided into members' voluntary and creditors' voluntary liquidations.

Members' voluntary winding up

This can only take place where the company concerned is thought to be solvent; it is thus going into liquidation simply because the shareholders wish either to close down and realize their investment or to continue the business in a different form. If it is proposed to go into members' voluntary liquidation the directors – or a majority of directors – must make a statutory declaration that they have made a full inquiry into the company's affairs and that the company is in a position to pay all its debts in full within twelve months. This is called a declaration of solvency and there are penalties for making a wrongful declaration.

If a creditor learns that one of his customers is going into members' voluntary liquidation he should usually be able to rely on receiving payment in full.

Creditors' voluntary winding up

This is the other form of voluntary winding up. Here the company must call a meeting of its creditors and present to them a statement of affairs with a list of the creditors' names and the amount owed to each one. Before this meeting the members (shareholders) of the company pass a resolution for the company to be voluntarily wound up and they may, if they wish, nominate a liquidator to carry out the work of realizing and distributing the assets of the company. The purpose of the creditors' meeting – which is presided over by a director of the company – is in effect to endorse the shareholders' resolution and nomination of a liquidator.

The creditors do not have to endorse these arrangements. They may wish to appoint an alternative liquidator in whom they have more confidence – if so the members must accept the creditors' nomination. Joint liquidators may be appointed. It is possible, however, that the creditors may be so dissatisfied with the state of affairs revealed that they refuse to endorse any voluntary winding-up proposals at all and instead make arrangements among themselves for a petition to be made to the court for a compulsory winding up. The matter will then be argued in court and a compulsory winding-up order may or may not be made.

It will be appreciated, therefore, that the creditors are in quite a strong position provided that a majority of them in number and amount can agree among themselves on the best course of action to be followed. It is possible, however, for the directors of the company to steamroller through their own arrangements (which may facilitate the concealment of fraudulent activities) by either of two means:

1   By being themselves unsecured creditors of the company for large amounts – for example, in respect of their loan accounts.
2   By means of proxy votes in favour of the chairman of the meeting sent in by unsuspecting creditors who do not attend the meeting in person.

To avoid either of these possibilities all unsecured creditors are best advised to:

1   Attend the meeting of creditors in person, if their involvement is significant, or, alternatively, to arrange to be represented by one of

the reputable trade-protection associations who as a rule make no charge whatsoever for this service.

2   On no account send in their completed proxy blank to the chairman of the meeting unless he is known to them and enjoys their complete confidence.

Before leaving the subject of voluntary liquidations it should be mentioned that the liquidator will, not unnaturally, have to be paid for his services. His remuneration may be fixed in advance as a certain sum or it may be arranged that he retain a fixed percentage of the value of the assets realized and distributed. If there are few realizable assets, the creditors will have to find his remuneration themselves and in these circumstances they will probably prefer not to appoint a liquidator but leave the liquidation with the Official Receiver.

Compulsory winding up

In the previous chapter it was shown that a creditor may, in certain circumstances, petition for a company to be compulsorily wound up by reason of its inability to pay its debts. The usual grounds for such a petition are a judgment debt, but a company is also deemed to be unable to pay its debts if a creditor, who is owed more than £50, serves on the debtor's registered office a demand under his hand requiring the debtor to pay the sum so due and the debtor neglects for a period of three weeks thereafter 'to pay the sum or to secure or compound for it to the reasonable satisfaction of the creditor'.

Other grounds for a petition need not be discussed here as they relate in the main to the rights of members of the company and are of little interest to creditors.

The court will hear the petition and the opposition to it, if any, and will decide on the evidence available whether to make a winding-up order, to dismiss the petition or adjourn it, or to make a conditional order. The more creditors who support the petition, the more likely the court will be to overrule possible objections from the directors and make a winding-up order. A creditor who sees a petition advertised against one of his debtors can serve notice of support for the petition. If the first petitioner is then paid off, a supporting petitioner can immediately substitute his claim and thus save both time and legal expense.

If the court makes a winding-up order, the company is required to submit to the Official Receiver a statement of its affairs. The Official Receiver will then make a report to the court stating whether in his opinion further inquiries should be made about the reason for the company's failure or whether other aspects of the company's history should be investigated. If appropriate, the court will arrange for these inquiries to be put in hand. The Official Receiver becomes the provisional liquidator of the company and he will call meetings of the company's creditors and its members at which it will be decided whether the court should be advised to appoint an outside liquidator or not. In the latter case the Official Receiver will become the liquidator.

The liquidator will then, under the court's supervision, proceed to realize the assets and distribute them to the various creditors.

Creditors' committees of inspection

If a liquidator other than the Official Receiver is appointed to a limited company, in either a voluntary or a compulsory winding up, a committee of inspection is usually appointed to assist and to some extent supervise the liquidation. This committee, consisting usually of three or five persons representing substantial creditors, is elected by the main body of creditors at the meeting. If it is a voluntary liquidation the members of the company may also nominate members of the committee subject to the creditors' approval.

The duties of the committee are to agree the liquidator's remuneration, to advise him on trade matters, and to audit his cash book periodically.

Undue or fraudulent preference

This is a complicated subject but must be mentioned briefly. If a debtor is insolvent it is a general principle of English law that no creditor should be preferred: the available assets should be shared out proportionately among creditors, subject to the prior claims of secured and preferential creditors. If a debtor attempts to pay off one creditor unfairly at the expense of the general body of creditors his action *may* amount to a fraudulent preference. The period during which such a payment might be held to be a fraudulent preference is up to six months before the act of bankruptcy in the case of a private individual and up to six months before a meeting of creditors in the case of a limited company. The effect of a fraudulent preference is to make the transaction in question voidable by, for example, the trustee in bankruptcy or liquidator applying to the court to have it reversed.

Whether a given action does in fact constitute a fraudulent preference is difficult to say in general terms, as even lawyers disagree on how the law should be interpreted. Where a debtor pays a pressing creditor there is almost certainly no fraudulent preference, although other older debts may remain unpaid. Where, however, a creditor *takes security* for his debt from the debtor within the six-month period – or twelve months where security takes the form of a floating charge – then there probably is a fradulent preference.

Should some suspicious action come to light within the six-month period, a creditor would be well advised to take legal advice immediately. It may be possible thereby to gain possession of assets for the general benefit of creditors which might otherwise be lost to them.

Receivers

If a debtor has given security to a bank or other financial institution, by means of a mortgage or charge over certain assets, the secured creditor may in certain circumstances – for example, default on the loan or the loan interest – have the power to enforce the charge and take possession of the assets so pledged. The same applies if the secured creditor holds a floating charge over all the assets of the business. In such circumstances the most usual way for a secured creditor to safeguard his interests is to appoint a receiver, usually but not always a practising chartered accountant. In most cases the loan agreement or 'debenture' will make a specific provision for such an appointment. Alternatively the receiver may be appointed by order of the court.

The object of the receiver's appointment is (*a*) to safeguard the security of the secured creditor and (*b*) to realize sufficient assets as quickly as possible to liquidate the secured debt. Once this has been done the receiver must withdraw and leave the remaining assets once more in the hands of the proprietors of the business.

Whether sufficient assets will remain after the withdrawal of a receiver to satisfy all or even part of the claims of unsecured creditors will depend on what is left: sometimes the debtor will be able to continue trading; more frequently a meeting of creditors will have to be held and the company will go into liquidation so that the remaining assets can be realized and shared out among the unsecured creditors. Sometimes the assets are insufficient to discharge even the secured indebtedness and unsecured creditors will thus not receive a penny. The dangers of giving credit to debtors where secured indebtedness exists have already been discussed.

So long as a receiver's appointment remains in force, neither the proprietors of the business nor its unsecured creditors can do very much to remove him, nor indeed have they any real say in the disposal of the assets which have been charged. They may feel that the assets are being realized too quickly and as a result are fetching a fraction of their real value. They can do nothing about this state of affairs so long as the receiver is acting within the terms of his debenture. They can go to law over the right of the debenture holder to appoint the receiver in the first place but this is not usually a fruitful course of action as the chances of defeating the form of, say, a bank's debenture are not great.

An unsecured creditor can still obtain judgment and petition for the debtor company to be wound up compulsorily. This may hinder a receiver somewhat but he still has the assets and may be able to transfer them into another company, leaving the wreck of the old company to go into liquidation. An unsecured creditor's best course of action is usually to wait and see how a receiver intends to act. A receiver must, within six months of his appointment, prepare and circulate to unsecured creditors a statement of affairs as at the date of his appointment.

It is usual for a receiver to continue the business while he is realizing the assets under his control. In such circumstances he may agree to pay cash for fresh goods or alternatively seek to purchase on credit terms. A supplier may, therefore, have to decide how much credit to give to a receiver. In this connection it is important to note that the receiver is a completely separate legal entity from the old debtor and he is *personally liable for everything for which he has signed an order and which has been delivered and invoiced to him.* When selling to a receiver it is vital, therefore, to ensure that a signed order has been obtained from him (or from a person specifically authorized to act on his behalf) and that the necessary invoice and statement is made out to the receiver. To avoid confusion with previous transactions for which the receiver is not liable (and which should be transferred to the doubtful debt ledger) a separate account in the name of the receiver should be opened.

As already mentioned, most receivers are practising chartered accountants and this should inspire confidence in prospective creditors. Receivers can be sued in a personal capacity for goods signed for by themselves and properly delivered and invoiced. Chartered accountants usually prove to be a fair trade risk but it is not unheard of for difficulty to be experienced in collecting from a receiver. Prospective creditors should therefore look closely at the receiver's own professional standing before granting substantial credit. One way of doing this is for the supplier to approach his own auditors to see if they know the receiver's firm. They certainly will not wish to go into writing on the subject but they may be prepared to say something off the record to set minds at rest.

Another point to consider before giving credit to a receiver is the standing of whoever appointed him. If the debenture holder is one of the clearing banks it is almost certain that arrangements will have been made to provide the receiver with sufficient funds for the proper execution of his duties. Finally, if nothing is known of the receiver's own standing or of the party appointing him it is advisable to get in touch with him personally before becoming further involved.

Moratoriums

Where a business finds itself in a seriously illiquid situation, it may approach its creditors and seek their agreement to a payments moratorium under which each creditor agrees not to press his claim for an agreed period in consideration of the other creditors holding off likewise. The object of the moratorium is, on the one hand, to prevent any creditor preferring himself in relation to the general body of creditors and, on the other hand, to gain time for the debtor to dispose of assets — usually stock — in an orderly way and so realize the maximum for the ultimate benefit of creditors generally.

Moratoriums do not have to take any particular form and are merely agreements between a debtor and his creditors. These arrangements may be informal but a creditor, unless extremely close to the debtor, would be wise to insist on some formality to ensure that the affairs of the business are handled properly for the duration of the moratorium. The minimum formalities which a creditor should insist on when faced with this situation are:

1 A proper statement of affairs should be circulated to all creditors.
2 A list of the major creditors involved (say those owed over £100) should be drawn up. A frank disclosure of the position is the very least which should be expected from a debtor who is seeking further time in this way.
3 The directors' loan accounts, if any, should be frozen until unsecured creditors have been paid in full or until the debtor goes into liquidation as the case may be. The directors of a limited company should be expected to subordinate their own unsecured claims to those of the outside creditors.
4 The bank account should be frozen (if it is overdrawn as it is likely to be) and a new account opened for the duration of the moratorium. All receipts and payments should be conducted through the new account and the surplus, as it accumulates, should be distributed to creditors (including the bank) in whatever way has been agreed beforehand.
5 A trustee appointed to supervise the moratorium generally and to countersign all cheques drawn on the new bank account. The trustee will usually be a professional man such as the debtor's auditor.

These measures should ensure that creditors in a moratorium obtain fair treatment.

The debtor may or may not have to pay interest on the extended credit which he is obtaining in this way. However, payment of interest in these circumstances seems rather pointless as it merely prolongs the moratorium. Money paid out in interest could instead be paid to reduce creditors' claims.

On occasion the smaller creditors are paid out in full, leaving a small number of the larger creditors in the moratorium. This makes the moratorium easier to operate and obviates the possibility of a small creditor 'rocking the boat' – that is, pressing for settlement of his claim in full instead of agreeing to the moratorium. Any creditor has a legal right to do this and a small creditor may judge that, if he does press his claim, the larger creditors may prefer to agree to his being paid out in full rather than let him wreck their efforts at salvaging part at least of their much larger involvement. To avoid such a situation the smaller creditors are frequently either paid off at once or paid off in the first distribution to creditors which might be arranged as follows: all debts up to (say) £50 in full plus 10 per cent of all creditor balances over and above.

It will be appreciated from the foregoing that no creditor need agree to a moratorium. He can instead press his claim and, if the debtor is a limited company, petition for it to be compulsorily wound up. Such a petition may be opposed and defeated by the other creditors as not in the general interest but it will nevertheless prove an embarrassment.

If the debtor is an individual or a firm, the moratorium constitutes a statutory act of bankruptcy on the basis of which bankruptcy proceedings could be started.

Bad-debt provisions

It is important that systematic provision should be made for bad debts as they arise. The object of such provisions is, first, to report the occurrence of the bad debt to management and, second, to write down by a realistic figure the control balance of the sales ledger so that the total of this important item in the balance sheet represents the true value of this asset.

There are two problems affecting bad-debt provisions: when and how much to provide. The trouble is that the earlier the provision is made the less accurate it is likely to be. The procedure will vary according to the size and nature of the business and the following comments are in the nature of general observations only.

Assuming that the responsibility for collecting the recoveries, if any, on bad debts is transferred from the credit manager to the company secretary, it is a good plan for those accounts to be transferred out of the sales ledger into a bad-debt ledger and provided for at the same point in time. Whether responsibility passes or not, a line must be drawn to indicate when provision should be made for a bad or doubtful debt. An account should be provided for as soon as the company receives a notice of a meeting of creditors, a petition for compulsory winding-up, a receiver's appointment, a bankruptcy petition or a moratorium as the case may be. Provision may also be made when legal proceedings are started against a debtor by the supplier's solicitors. Alternatively, it may be found in certain trades that the majority of accounts passed to the solicitors are paid in full and within a short space of time, in which case a better plan is to make provision only for those accounts still unpaid, say, four weeks after legal proceedings have been started. The important point is that whatever rule is made it should be clear and easily operated.

The second problem is how much to provide. A company may make specific or general provisions (or both) for bad debts. Specific provisions, provided they are reasonable, are allowable expenses for the purposes of tax computation, whereas a general provision is likely to be regarded by the Revenue as more in the nature of a reserve and is not usually allowable. It is, therefore, sensible from every point of view to make the fullest reasonable provision against specified bad or doubtful debts.

At the time specific provisions are first made the amount to be provided can be assessed by the credit manager or other responsible officer of the company. Alternatively, all such specific debts may be fully provided automatically, subject to being reviewed at the end of the company's financial year. By this time, more facts concerning individual debts will have come to light and more accurate assessments of the amount of the anticipated recovery can be made.

For the purposes of making specific provisions the entire bad-debt ledger should be reviewed annually, around the time of the end of the financial year, and the prospects of recovery on each significant debt should be reassessed in the light of the latest information. Small bad debts should be fully provided – the time spent by management in assessing the recovery prospects of such debts is not worth the small difference any such calculation would contribute to the state of the balance sheet. The more significant bad debts should also be provided in full except where there is some definite evidence that a recovery may reasonably be anticipated.

In practical terms, the quickest and usually the best way to achieve this aim is to take the total of the bad-debt control account and deduct from it the value of specified anticipated recoveries, erring always on the side of caution. Thus a list of net bad debts – that is, gross bad debts minus anticipated recoveries – can be produced for the inspection of the auditors and the Tax Inspector should he require this information. The auditors will certainly require to satisfy themselves that reasonable provision has been made for all debts which may subsequently prove irrecoverable.

CHAPTER 10

Credit Insurance

Whereas in some trades the credit risk is so low that the question of insurance hardly arises, in other trades there is what might be termed a high endemic risk. The toy trade was once considered to be steady and traditional – dolls, teddy bears, toy soldiers and model ships have appealed to generations of children. With the coming of television serials a new dimension of risk has entered the picture: demand for the latest toy is now created almost overnight and at the end of the serial the demand wanes with almost equal rapidity; the stockist who is left with these high-fashion goods faces loss unless sufficient profit has been made on the previous sales. The same principle has applied in certain areas of the textile trade ever since 'fashion' was invented.

Risk factor

There is a great temptation to cash in on a popular fashion and the man who guesses right may make enormous profits. Few experts are, however, infallible and they need the large profits from the successful coups to compensate for the inevitable losses which follow up a sudden change of fashion, whether it be in clothes, toys, or any other commodity. Exactly the same principle applies in trades where there is a high research or development factor. Much research and development must by its nature be profitless and, therefore, when it is profitable it requires to be highly profitable. This may be all very well if large capital resources are available but these endemic hazards do not seem to deter the adventurous with little or no capital from joining in the fun. In fact, the man who can establish credit for himself without capital in a risk-bound trade is on to a good thing. If he guesses right he makes a fortune and if he guesses wrong his creditors foot the bill. This situation is, of course, not so good for the creditors and it is one of the reasons for the success of trade credit insurance whereby, for a relatively small percentage of their profit, creditors can obtain insurance to cover the risk of bad debts − the *del credere* risk.

Risk spread

Another factor to be considered is the risk spread of the business. If a company has a large number of smallish debtors it is well spread, whereas if it has a small number of large debtors it is not well spread. In the latter case the likelihood of a loss being sustained may be much less but conversely, were it to occur, its impact would be much greater and possibly cataclysmic. No business should be owed so much by one debtor that it could not itself survive that debtor's failure, however unlikely. To be in such a position is to be in a position of weakness rather than master of one's fate.

So much for theory: it is unfortunately true that many companies do depend to a large extent on too few major customers for their livelihood and they would do well to take out an insurance policy to cover the credit risk. Credit insurance also has much to offer the well-spread business unless the business is so well spread that it may rightly be deemed self-insuring. Of companies obliged to grant trade credit this can be truly said only of a small minority.

Worry, or its absence, plays an incalculable part in the success of any business enterprise. This item does not appear in any balance sheet. A worried man generally has less confidence than his more relaxed counterpart and he is more likely to buckle under stress or to take the wrong decision. Worried men usually take the short-term view while confident men can take a longer view and ride out a short-term setback. Credit insurance relieves at least one source of worry even for those who rarely suffer bad debts for, paradoxically, it is those who least often suffer that are hit hardest when the blow falls. There are few blows so sickening as to work hard for a whole year to build up a retained profit of, say, £3,000 and then find that a debtor for a similar amount has been unable to meet his liabilities and has called a meeting of creditors. Credit insurance eliminates this possibility.

Market intelligence

Quite apart from all these considerations, one of the chief causes of bad-debt losses arises from ignorance of the market. Most professional businessmen will not admit such ignorance of the home market, yet they are quite prepared to admit it when it comes to exports. Perhaps they have appointed a new agent in an overseas market of which they have no previous experience and they know their agent only by reputation. In such circumstances it is not only prudent but also commonplace to seek export credit insurance – this subject is dealt with in this and the succeeding chapter. What is not so readily understood is that home markets are undergoing constant changes which may be so gradual as to be almost imperceptible.

The man who may have known his market ten years ago does not necessarily know it now unless he has taken pains to keep himself up to date. For instance, during the first half of the twentieth century many more people went to work on a bicycle, but what is happening now? What has changed is the volume of motor traffic, the congestion on the roads, and the sheer danger to the cyclist. The bicycle used to be an efficient, safe, and pleasant means of transport. Owing to circumstances beyond the would-be cyclists' control, it is no longer true. This has adversely affected those in the cycle trade. However, more and more people are taking up gardening, thus sales of garden tools have been rising steadily. The bicycle manufacturer or repairer who has diversified into lawn mowers may, therefore, be doing very well whereas had he stayed with bicycles alone this could hardly be expected. This rather obvious example serves to illustrate that it is not enough just to know all about bicycles, or any other single commodity, in isolation from the many other factors that affect its marketability and hence the financial health of those engaged in that market.

It is the job of the credit insurer to be up to date at all times and in all matters which concern the financial health of the accounts he is insuring.

Credit-insurance market

Brokers and underwriters

Like other insurance markets credit insurers are divided into brokers and underwriters. The advantage of employing a broker is that – if he does his job properly – he can give impartial advice about which is the best type of credit insurance policy for the business. He should also possess sufficient knowledge to be able to ensure that a quotation is reasonable. A broker is reimbursed for his services by commission which is paid by the underwriter. It does not cost the businessman any more to consult a broker than to approach the underwriter direct.

The most important consideration in all insurance matters is integrity and this applies equally to credit insurance. It is, therefore, preferable to approach an underwriter of undoubted integrity than to employ a broker about whom there are any doubts whatsoever. The fact that a broker has superficially no particular axe to grind is no guarantee of his integrity nor is there any guarantee that he will introduce his clients to the soundest underwriter, especially if he is obtaining an exceptional rate of commission. This situation is sometimes accompanied by cut-price premiums which should also be regarded with the utmost circumspection. Insurance which does not pay up when the calamity occurs is a complete waste of money whether because the insurance company has no funds or because the 'small print' relieves it of its moral obligations.

A marginal difference in premium quoted should, therefore, rank low in the selection of insurance policies. What is far more important is the financial strength of the insurance company, the amount of cover it is prepared to give and, perhaps most important, its reputation in dealing with reasonable claims. From this it emerges that the most important factor in credit insurance is having a policy underwritten by a company of undoubted integrity. This can be obtained without going through a broker. However, there are many such companies of integrity and a good broker may well be able to give sound advice about which is the best of a number of good alternatives.

Operation of trade-credit insurance

The method of operation will depend on which type of credit-insurance organization is providing the policy. At the time of writing there are three types of operation: the ordinary trade-credit insurance company as typified by Trade Indemnity Company Limited; the ECGD policy provided by the Export Credits Guarantee Department; and the without-recourse factoring policy which caters for both home trade and exports. All of these reserve the right to refuse credit cover altogether on certain names and all reserve the right to decline excessive amounts of cover on certain names. It is prudent to establish in principle from the outset the extent of the cover that will be provided and what the premium will be. In principle all of them require all of a company's turnover to be offered. The insured is not permitted to select against the insurer. If this were allowed not only would insuring become hazardous in itself but premiums would soar.

As the credit-insurance market has gained in experience, so it has become more flexible in its approach to credit problems and in certain cases and for good reasons it may be possible to exclude certain markets or merchandise or customers from the whole turnover cover by agreement with the underwriters. Alternatively, it may also be possible to insure specified accounts to the exclusion of all other accounts. These exceptions, however, do not invalidate the soundness of the general principles outlined above.

Credit-insurance companies

In the case of pure credit insurance it is normally necessary to submit a list of customers with a note of the maximum amount of credit required on each. This list is then approved or amended by the underwriters and stands until such time as either:

1   The underwriter notifies the insured of a change in the amount of cover given on an insured name; or
2   The insured seeks increased cover on a given name or submits new names.

In cases where a large company with a wide spread of relatively small debtors of repute is concerned, the underwiters may give some discretion to the insured. They may, for instance, agree that any customer whose name appears in a work of credit reference for a certain amount, may be granted that amount of credit without specific reference to the underwriter. This, of course, imposes an obligation on the insured to take reasonable care. For instance, he may be required to obtain satisfactory trade references on new customers or to obtain other types of credit information which support the decision to grant credit.

The insured must also take all reasonable steps to collect overdue accounts and he will be required to report to the underwriters at regular intervals on the state of his overdue accounts. Failure to take reasonable precautions in both credit checking and in collection of overdue accounts may prejudice claims and this is reasonable if loss arises from contributory negligence on the part of the insured.

These various requirements are clearly laid out in print by the underwriters who do expect the insured to exercise exactly the same degree of care as he would exercise were he not insuring his debts. Provided this care is exercised the underwriters will normally pay any claim up to the percentage agreed in the contract unless the issue is clouded by a merchandise dispute, for the credit-insurance companies do not cover the insured against the risk of his own shortcomings or errors. The insurance cover is confined to the risk of the customer failing to pay within a specified period after the due date for payment, provided always there is no valid contractual reason for non-payment.

The percentage cover must also be clearly understood as well as the cost of the premium which is commonly expressed as a percentage of turnover. For example, a quotation of 25p per cent for 80 per cent cover may be offered and accepted. Assume then that a specific name has been insured for £1,000 and that this also is the amount of the unpaid debt. The cover on this £1,000 will have cost £2.50 and the pay-out will be 80 per cent of the loss – that is, £800 if the loss is total. If the failed debtor pays a dividend of 20p in the £, the total loss will be £800 and the insurance company will meet 80 per cent of that – that is, £640. In practice the underwriters may pay the insured £800 and stand in for the whole dividend. If they subsequently recover 20p in the £ on the whole debt of £1,000, this will mean a recovery of £200 and they will normally pass on 20 per cent of this £40 to the insured which comes to the same thing.

If the insured despatches goods to a greater value than the agreed cover, he will be uninsured on the excess. Therefore, in the example quoted above, if he had despatched, say, £1,500 he would still only receive from the insurance company 80 per cent of the insured part after the appropriate part of the dividend, if any, had been credited.

It follows from this that if the insured wished to despatch goods in excess of the cover figure he should approach the underwriters for additional cover either on a temporary or a semi-permanent basis. In practice it is quite common for underwriters to grant a temporary increase in cover, lasting perhaps three months, to meet such situations. It is a matter for regret that a number of insured, either do not bother to ask or, having asked, ignore the answer and thereby incur unnecessary loss.

In addition to the provision of credit insurance, the underwriting company conducts an active and effective debt-collection service on behalf of its clients at quite nominal charges. This service does not, like the factor's service, cover all debts, but relates to the overdue accounts which the client wishes the underwriter to collect and which might otherwise fall due for payment under the terms of the insured's policy with the underwriters. The provision of this additional service mitigates the likelihood of loss.

The services of the credit-insurance companies are not confined to the domestic market. They also offer their clients insurance for export transactions, as well as an overseas debt-collection service. This is obtained through the International Credit Insurance Association which operates through a widespread network of correspondents. However, the cover is not so extensive as that provided by the ECGD.

It should be remembered that one of the great values of a credit insurance policy is that, in addition to safeguarding actual bad-debt loss, it affords access to a pool of credit knowledge that is probably not otherwise available. If the underwriters decline a risk or reduce the amount of cover they are prepared to give, they do so for a good reason. After all, such decisions reduce their own premium income. No one has yet devised a way of measuring how much potential loss is avoided by declining bad business in the first place and this is one of the most useful, if unsung, attributes of credit insurance.

Export Credits Guarantee Department

The ECGD operates along comparable lines to those outlined in the previous section. However, credit terms are generally more varied and longer in the export market.

Shipments policies and contracts policies

A shipments policy is generally cheaper because the ECGD does not come on risk until the goods are shipped whereas under a contracts policy it comes on risk when the manufacturing process starts. This latter point is of particular importance to companies that are manufacturing a custom-built article for a special purpose required possibly only by one particular customer. If the customer goes out of business before manufacture is completed and it is not possible to place the goods with another customer the value of this insurance will be appreciated.

Again the ECGD will require the proposed credit to be notified to and approved by it. The Department may suggest that a discretionary amount of credit judgment is left to their insured whereby he may ship goods up to a certain agreed limit to any customer provided always he has first obtained satisfactory credit information to justify such a decision.

The amount of cover granted will vary according to the terms of the contract but some policies are written with cover up to 95 per cent of the eventual loss. The premium will vary not only according to the nature of the business but, more particularly, according to the export market's own standing.

The ECGD not only provides cover against the insolvency of an overseas buyer but also covers certain war, political, and exchange risks. This is particularly valuable when, for instance, an overseas government refuses exchange-control permission for the buyer to pay his UK supplier or, alternatively, permits payment only in blocked funds.

Whereas most domestic trade is conducted on open account and in accordance with the normal trade terms which, in the majority of trades, means monthly terms, the terms of the export trade vary greatly and careful attention must be given to correct documentation and despatch. When application is made to the ECGD for cover, the terms must be stated as well as the amount of credit required. The ECGD may approve the application as submitted or it may make certain special conditions. For example, it may decline £1,000 on open account to a certain buyer but it may approve the same amount on CAD terms that is, where the documents of title to the goods must be sent to a bank in the buyer's country with instructions to hand over the documents only against payment in cash by the buyer.

Even CAD has its problems if the buyer has no cash or chooses not to take up the documents. Arrangements may then have to be made to ship the goods back or dispose of them in the local market at the best price obtainable before they deteriorate and become valueless. Provided the ECGD agreed to insure this transaction on CAD terms it will of course bear the agreed percentage of the resultant end loss, but what of the case when the documents are despatched by mistake direct to the end buyer who thus obtains titles without having to disgorge cash? It is quite surprising how often this elementary mistake is made in exporters' despatch and documentation departments. In such circumstances the underwriter is under neither contractual nor moral obligation to pay a claim since the specified conditions were ignored by the insured. This example may help to illustrate the importance of following correct export documentation procedure irrespective of whether the credit risk is insured.

Credit insurance through factoring

Factors generally provide a four-part service to their clients which consists of:

1   Sales ledger accounting.
2   Debt collection.
3   Credit insurance.
4   Immediate payment against sales invoices.

Obviously it is more expensive than credit insurance on its own and there is only one satisfactory test of whether it is worth the additional cost — that is, whether at the end of the year the client will have made a greater profit by virtue of the fact that he factored his sales. Some factors do not provide credit insurance and their service may be aptly described as 'recourse factoring'. They, therefore, do not come within the scope of this chapter.

Companies which factor sales without recourse to their clients fulfil the same function as credit-insurance companies because this is an integral part of the service offered. The method of operation is essentially different for a variety of practical reasons. The factor insures all debts which have his prior approval. Because the factor operates his clients' sales ledgers he has the precise position of all customers' accounts continuously available and, by the same token, the supplier of the goods does not have them available. It is, therefore, neither practicable nor desirable to operate on a system of credit limits but rather on current credit requirements in the light of current payments performance. Limits would be of little use to the factored client since he is probably not aware of how much is still owing by any particular customer, nor should he worry about this because he has transferred this responsibility to the factor.

Instead factors have devised a series of shipping codes which enable their clients to despatch at regular intervals normal amounts of goods to approved customers without prior reference to the factor. Despatches of exceptional size or to new customers or to overdue customers will not come within these arrangements and specific approval for these credit risks must be sought. This method has somewhat more flexibility than the fixed-limit system but this can, of course, cut both ways. The tendency should be for the most satisfactory accounts to have the most lenient control while less satisfactory accounts will receive less generous treatment. The factor's aim is to get away from the limit concept and concentrate instead on the concept of reasonable credit requirements at any given moment.

Because the factor actually carries out the sales book-keeping and collection work, he is in direct contact with the debtor or buyer and can establish a friendly rapport which can engender mutual confidence. Not only does this facilitate flexibility in control of credit but it justifies the factor in offering his clients 100 per cent credit cover which is not usually, if ever, obtainable from other credit-insurance organizations which do not enjoy this advantage. This means that the supplier is able to insure his profit as well as his costs.

In addition the factor guarantees payment in full on a pre-determined fixed date which is calculated on an average of the time taken by customers to settle their accounts. The supplier thus knows exactly when he will receive payment, always provided the debt is not disputed. This is an extremely useful bonus peculiar to the factoring contract. Other forms of credit insurance will pay at a point of time when the inability of the buyer to pay has been factually established or, alternatively, a set number of months after due date according to the terms of the policy. Thus, although the debt may be insured, some months will usually elapse before the claim is paid and interest on the sum outstanding is not insured. The factor will, therefore, give a higher percentage of cover and will pay more promptly as he is obliged to under the factoring contract.

A number of factoring companies specialize in assisting exporters. To do this effectively they must have access to credit men in the buyer's country. While some favour a network of correspondents, as is not uncommon in banking circles, others favour establishing associated companies in the main markets of the world. It is usual for the factoring company in the buyer's country to underwrite the credit risk because it is this company which is making the credit judgment. However, this need not concern the British exporter who elects to factor his overseas sales as his contract will be with the factoring company in his own country from whom he will receive all the payments for his exports.

This arrangement not only enables the exporter to enjoy complete credit cover but also to dispense with sales ledgering and collection work which may be even more difficult to organize when foreign currencies are involved. The exporter must first obtain the factor's credit approval (but need not seek out credit information) and he also has to raise the invoices and carry out the necessary documentation in relation to the goods themselves. He despatches the invoices and documents and sends a copy of each invoice to the factor. Trade disputes apart, the exporter's problems end here. He receives payment at a fixed date and he may also be afforded a drawing facility whereby he can borrow in advance of the debt maturity date. The factor is responsible for obtaining settlement from the buyer and carrying the liability if he fails to do so.

Cost of trade-credit insurance

It is impossible to lay down any hard and fast rules of costing, let alone compare the costs of these differing services. Credit-insurance companies and the ECGD both provide sound insurance and good advice but this does not mean that their clients can dispense with credit management or sales ledgering and collection work.

As a very rough guide, a safe trade on short credit terms to an established and highly reputable market may cost less than $\frac{1}{8}$ per cent for 85 to 90 per cent cover, whereas a more hazardous trade to less reliable markets may cost $\frac{3}{4}$ per cent for only 50 per cent cover, particularly if long terms are involved, and it should be remembered that $\frac{3}{4}$ per cent for 50 per cent cover is equivalent to $1\frac{1}{2}$ per cent for 100 per cent cover. Special rates will obviously apply to cases involving longer-term credit or to markets where there are exceptional credit hazards. So far as exporting is concerned, factors are well placed to handle transactions on short-term credit on either documentary terms or on open account. The ECGD, on the other hand, is better placed when it comes to longer-term credit insurance or trade with countries where factors are not established.

As factors quote for the service as a whole, it is not possible to state what part of their fee is attributable to this one aspect. In addition to the risk assessment, the fee depends upon the turnover handled, the average invoice value, and hence the volume of sales ledger and collection work in relation to the turnover and also, curiously, the volume of credit notes and disputes. If a trade is disputatious, the factor cannot help becoming involved and this increases his costs of operation. Thus the overall charge made by a factor for the total service may vary from as little as ½ per cent to as much as 2½ per cent of turnover, depending upon his assessment of all the relevant factors and, out of this, the credit insurance|element alone may be as little as ¼ per cent or as much as ¾ per cent but this is, of course, for 100 per cent cover.

Is credit insurance worth while? There are few trades in which the answer can be other than in the affirmative. Furthermore, there is no question of any reputable company demanding excessive or unreasonable premiums. The more difficult question to answer is whether factoring companies are worth the difference and this will depend entirely on the circumstances of the company seeking insurance. The factor is ready to make advances at from 2 to 3 per cent over base rate, to enable his client to pay his own suppliers more promptly for best discount. Much expense will be saved by the removal of the sales ledger and its whole operation. The need to engage an experienced credit manager is obviated. In the case of exports, the existence of an associate company on the buyer's ground enables the buyer to pay locally and raise queries in his own language with someone who is there and will understand. Many problems can be dealt with promptly before they have grown into disputes.

Nevertheless, a large company with a well-established sales administration and credit management and with ample financial resources may have relatively little to gain from factoring and is better advised to consider credit insurance on its own. Another company may find that, while it can make use of the factor's services with advantage, the additional cost is not likely to be recouped from increased profits and it, too, would be better advised to have just a credit-insurance policy.

However, this still leaves a large number of companies whose administrative capacity has not grown in relation to their sales, or which do not possess the knowledge necessary to break successfully into a new market, or whose operations are not yet sufficiently large to sustain the necessary administrative overheads to back the sales. Such companies may find the more expensive package deal cheaper than any alternative. In other words, factoring is for those who will profit from it.

CHAPTER 11

Export Credit

Selling to far distant customers has its problems. Contact is less frequent, communication is more difficult and more expensive, foreign exchange is a problem, the legal and commercial background may be quite different and what is an acceptable level of behaviour in one country may differ materially from the code of conduct in another.

Clearly these considerations add to the problem of granting credit abroad but the exporter has two further problems to consider which do not arise in domestic transactions: how to guard against payments being blocked or otherwise prohibited by the government overseas (the political or transfer risk) and how to make sure that payment when it is received is as much as was originally anticipated (the exchange risk).

Historical development

Britain has been a major exporting nation for centuries but the pattern of exports has completely changed over the last 50 years and is still changing today with membership of the EEC.

The product has changed. Where once Britain exported coal, manufactured cotton goods, simple iron products, ships and railway equipment, today more and more of the nation's trade is in complex engineering products and consumer goods requiring considerable marketing investment.

The markets have changed. Fifty years ago almost all of Britain's exports went to the British Empire where English law, British commercial practices, British banks, insurance companies and shippers all operated – and almost everyone spoke English. More recently, with the disappearance of Imperial Preference, the immensely wealthy but highly competitive markets of Europe and North America have become more important. The currencies have changed. The currency of the British Empire was sterling. The Bank of England in London made certain that any local currencies were tied to sterling so there was no exchange problem for the British exporter to the British Empire. Today the British exporter who is selling to, say, Sweden is competing against German, French, Italians, not to mention an extremely efficient local industry. It is not surprising, therefore, if the customers in Sweden prefer to be invoiced in their own currency. But what will Sw.Kr.50,000 on today's invoice be worth in three months time when the customer pays? Will the exporter make an ultimate profit or a loss as a result of the fluctuations in exchange?

The terms of sale have changed. In the tied Imperial markets international trade was in the hands of internationally known business houses and if the exporter was not dealing through this medium he would normally sell on the basis of a letter of credit. This eliminated the credit risk and the exchange risk. A Swedish customer is unlikely to buy on letter of credit if his Italian and German suppliers are offering 90 days open account. The British exporter cannot be competitive without offering open account credit to most of his customers throughout Europe and North America.

However, even if Britian's export markets are mainly new, and the traditional methods of making international settlements have changed, British businessmen have inherited some very valuable institutions.

The banks

First there are the banks. The British exporter is fortunate that perhaps the widest and best developed overseas banking system operates out of London. Although banking standards throughout the world may vary, the service of the British overseas banks conforms to the highest traditions of the British domestic banking system. These overseas banks can provide market intelligence, bank references, documentary credits and transmission of funds throughout the world. Historically rooted in the old Empire and Colonies they are today pushing into Europe and

North America. The exporter's own clearing or Scottish bank will be happy to put him in touch with whichever overseas bank can best help him in the market concerned.

The ECGD

The next most important institution, although not the oldest, is the Export Credits Guarantee Department or ECGD. This is a Department of the British government answering to the Secretary of State for Trade and Industry. The ECGD provides to exporters of British goods a variety of export credit guarantees or, in simple terms, credit insurance. Its importance can be judged by the fact that in 1970 no less than 36 per cent of all UK exports were insured with the ECGD and the proportion is growing.

As was shown in chapter 10, the ECGD provides exporters with a choice of a 'shipments' policy and a 'contracts' policy. The first covers the exporter from the moment he despatches his goods until he is paid and is rather cheaper than the contracts policy where the cover runs from the time that the contract of sale is finalized. This latter type of policy is designed to cover specialized goods – particularly large industrial plant which is being made to the customer's order and which cannot easily be disposed of elsewhere.

Cover is provided for sales on short 'monthly' terms up to in excess of five years credit for certain types of exports and where such terms are being offered by foreign competitors.

The cost of ECGD cover for most exports depends on the export market (there are four categories of market for premium purposes) and on the length of the credit being allowed. Specific policies for expensive capital goods are usually rated individually. For normal short-term business the *average* cost is 0.24 per cent but for specific long-term contracts the cost is greater. Cover is granted up to 90 per cent of the buyer (credit) risk and 90 to 95 per cent of political and transfer risks. Although the ECGD prefers to issue a 'comprehensive' policy covering all exports, it is also possible to negotiate a 'specific' policy excluding sales to certain markets provided that what is offered for insurance constitutes an acceptable mix to the insurers.

A useful by-product of the exporters' ECGD policy is access to cheap bank finance in approved cases. Under the Comprehensive Bill Guarantee scheme a policyholder of at least 12 months standing holding bills or promissory notes accepted by insured export debtors may discount this paper with his clearing or Scottish bank at ½ per cent over base rate (mininum 4½ per cent). The paper must have less than two years to maturity and the ECGD will fix a maximum limit to this discount facility. This is a valuable concession to exporters selling on bill of exchange terms. To cater for the exporter selling on open account terms up to six months the ECGD will, in approved cases, guarantee a bank loan to the exporter of up to 90 per cent of the value of the insured sales. The loan is secured by the promissory notes of the exporter who again must have held a comprehensive policy for at least 12 months to qualify for the same concessionary rate of interest.

For exports on medium term (over two years) the ECGD will in approved cases issue its guarantee to an exporter's bank which will then be able to finance the transaction at between 6 and 7 per cent plus a 1 per cent commitment fee.

Export merchants and confirming houses

Next there are the export merchant houses and confirming houses. These are, in the main, City of London institutions, some being bank owned, others independent of banks. Their function is to take the risk out of exporting either, in the case of the merchants, by buying the goods concerned for cash and reselling them in the foreign market or by negotiating, particularly with certain countries, package export deals involving credit and ECGD facilities from which individual exporters can benefit. The confirming houses' traditional role is that of opening (confirming) letters of credit for importers of British goods abroad. The British exporter can arrange to receive payment in cash on production of the shipping documents. Both the merchants' and confirming houses' traditional markets are the old Empire plus South America and the Far East, but they are now developing their service in Europe and for years have been active on the East Coast of North America.

More details of their services can be obtained from British Export Houses Association, 69 Cannon Street, London EC4.

Factoring

Finally there are the factors. Factoring companies originated from *del credere* agents of British exporters in the old American colonies who gave up chasing after orders and started instead guaranteeing their customers' credit and providing cash payment to the suppliers on receipt of invoices.

Following the Declaration of Independence, the Americans imposed a tariff on European imports so as to stimulate local industry and the factors found a ready demand for their services and finance among what was then a chronically undercapitalized economy. Factoring remained a purely American phenomenon until as recently as 1960 when the first of a number of European factoring companies was set up. Some of these function as 'groups' or 'chains' with the factoring company in one country (the export factor), transferring debts to his associate or affiliated factor in another country (the import factor) where the ultimate customer resides. Thus the local import factor is well placed to ascertain the credit standing of his local debtors and an exporter can avail himself of detailed financial knowledge regarding his customers in just about every developed market in the world and still deal only with one factoring company in his own locality.

As with the original American factoring companies, these new 'international' factors guarantee 100 per cent payment of sales which they have 'credit approved', provide a local collection service for invoices which are not paid promptly on due date and will usually provide finance for the exporter up to 80 per cent of the value of his export invoices if this is required.

A valuable by-product of the factor's service is quicker settlement of open account transactions because the follow-up of overdue payments and queries is carried out locally in the customer's country and in his own language thus minimizing both misunderstandings and delays.

Terms of sale

As with domestic trade the selection of the correct terms of sale is an important part of the management of export credit.

The most safe — but least competitive — way in which to deal is to ask the customer to open an irrevocable letter of credit confirmed by a London bank. This involves giving no credit to the customer whatever. On receipt of the letter of credit the first thing the exporter should do is read it carefully. A typical letter of credit is shown in Figure 11:1. It will be seen that if I. M. Careful Ltd presents the specified shipping documents together with its bill of exchange drawn on the customer to

The London Bank Ltd
Mansion House Square
London EC3 1ZZ

1 February 1973

I. M. Careful Ltd
61 London Road
Croynge

Dear Sirs

Confirmed Credit No 2021

We confirm to you that on the instructions of the Bank of Barataria we
have opened a credit in your favour for the sum of £2,000 (two
thousand pounds sterling) available for 60-day drafts drawn on us to be
accompanied by the following documents:

1   Full set clean 'on board' bills of lading
2   4 copies commercial invoice
3   Certificate of origin
4   2 copies marine war risk insurance policies
5   Consular invoice

evidencing shipment of 25 tape recorders from London not later than
15 March 1973 to Abdul & Co., Barataria.
        We undertake to honour all drafts drawn within the terms of
this credit provided such drafts bear the number and date of this credit.
        This credit expires 1 April 1973.

Yours faithfully

The London Bank Ltd

Figure 11:1 Specimen letter of credit

the London bank specified in the letter, that bank will pay the cash
value of the goods.
        A note of caution should be sounded. The documents must be in
perfect order. If the invoices are required in triplicate, *payment will be
withheld* if only two copies are presented until either a third copy is
produced or amended instructions are cabled to the London bank from
its overseas correspondent on whose behalf they are acting. In this

example the documents can easily be put right with the aid of a good office copier. A more serious problem arises if the letter requires a full set of bills of lading evidencing shipment ex-London to, say, the Seychelles by 31 December. It is possible that no ship is sailing for the Seychelles from the time the letter is opened until well into January. In such a case the exporter must arrange with his customer for the letter of credit to be amended by cable. So I. M. Careful Ltd reads the letter of credit carefully on receipt to make sure it can comply with all its terms.

If an exporter engages in any regular sales on letter of credit it can be seen that at least one clerk must have a good working knowledge of these procedures. However, the rules are quite straightforward and the foreign-counter staff of any local clearing or Scottish bank will advise the exporter as necessary.

The use of letters of credit varies from market to market: in some markets – for example, Japan – they are commonplace; in other markets their use is rare.

The next safest way of dealing with an export customer is on a 'cash against documents' basis (CAD). Here the full set of shipping documents (invoice, certificate of origin, packing list, insurance certificate, bills of lading or airway bill) are parcelled up with a sight bill of exchange (see Figure 11:2) and handed to the exporter's local bank with the instructions that the documents be forwarded to the

No 655 PAYABLE AT THE UNITED BANK OF LIMAGUSTA LTD, PO BOX 2000, LIMAGUSTA
EXCHANGE FOR   £219.90   4th January   1973

At SIGHT   *pay this* FIRST   *Bill of Exchange*
SECOND UNPAID   *to the Order of*

I.m. CAREFUL LIMITED, 61 LONDON ROAD, CROYNGE
Two hundred and nineteen pounds, ninety pence

Payable at the current rate of exchange for drafts drawn on London,

together with all stamp and collection charges.

Value RECEIVED   *which place to Account*

To   C. H. MOMODOPOULOS
       PO BOX 9000
       LIMAGUSTA   for and on behalf of
       CYPRUS   I. M. CAREFUL LIMITED

Figure 11:2 Bill of exchange payable at sight

customer's bank and released to the customer only when he pays the bill. The customer cannot take possession of the goods without the documents of title and therefore the exporter keeps control over the goods.

If goods are being consigned CAD by parcel post they should *not* be addressed to the customer as they may well be delivered if the local customs authorities are not too particular. Instead the goods should be consigned to the bank to which the documents of title are being forwarded.

Perhaps the main hazard of dealing on a CAD basis in some parts of the world is that importers may order goods on CAD and then not trouble to take up the documents. When the exporter has used every means at his disposal to induce the importer into taking up the documents without success, the exporter may decide to have the goods auctioned locally and the proceeds remitted home rather than go to the trouble of shipping them all the way back again. The original importer than steps up and, with the collusion of his friends, buys the goods he originally ordered for a fraction of their value. It is at this point that the value of a letter of credit becomes apparent.

It may be that I. M. Careful has been dealing with Abdul & Co for some considerable time on a CAD basis and the customer requests a little credit. No problems have ever occurred, an excellent supplier/customer arrangement exists and I. M. Careful wants to encourage his customer to increase his turnover. The best course is to send the next parcel of documents with a bill of exchange payable not at sight but at, say, 60 days after sight (D/A 60 days). (See Figure 11:3.) The collecting bank will arrange for the bill to be accepted and then hold it and present it in due course for payment. Abdul & Co. get their extra credit and I. M. Careful has the security of an accepted bill in the hands of the bank which will be self-collecting. There is the danger that the bill may be dishonoured. This is the same risk that I. M. Careful runs when giving credit anywhere or, if anything, rather less as doubtless I. M. Careful has instructed the bank that if any bill is not honoured it should be noted and protested with a view to bringing an immediate legal action for recovery of the money. The rules governing bills of exchange and letters of credit are universal and no special local legal knowledge is required. However, courts of law may or may not be corrupt and/or inefficient in different countries and this hazard is difficult tò quantify.

Trade has been conducted for centuries on this CAD or D/A basis. It

NO 655 PAYABLE AT THE UNITED BANK OF LIMAGUSTA LTD, PO BOX 2000 LIMAGUSTA
EXCHANGE FOR   £219.90   4th JANUARY   *19* 73

At   60 DAYS AFTER SIGHT   *pay this* FIRST   *Bill of Exchange*

SECOND UNPAID   *to the Order of*

I. M. CAREFUL, 61 LONDON ROAD, CROYNGE

Two hundred and nineteen pounds, ninety pence

Payable at the current rate of exchange for drafts drawn on London,

together with all stamp and collection charges.

Value RECEIVED   *which place to Account*

To   C. H. MOMODOPOULOS
           PO BOX 90000
           LIMAGUSTA   for and on behalf of
           CYPRUS   I. M. CAREFUL LIMITED

Figure 11:3 Bill of exchange payable 60 days after sight

is simple and relatively safe. The only problem is the time factor. Where
once goods were consigned on a slow cargo boat and the documents
sent out 10 days later by fast mail steamer so as to reach the port of
discharge first, today many goods are sent by airfreight, container, or
even by I. M. Careful's own delivery vans via the roll-on/roll-off
Continental ferry. This means that unless the goods are going halfway
round the world, they will reach their destination even weeks before
the documents. The goods cannot be cleared and quayside rent
(demurrage) starts to accumulate, thus the use of D/A and CAD terms
is becoming less common for exports to Europe and North America.
The documents are too slow in preparation and transmission. Instead,
sales are made on open account as with domestic trade and the
problems here are as described in Chapter 5, but there are a number of
noteworthy differences particularly with regard to due dates and
discounts.

First of all, the terms of sale should be clearly established. The
exporter says his terms are 60 days from despatch – the importer says
his terms are 60 days from receipt. If transport and clearance through
customs takes on average 14 days, there is an immediate argument over
the exact due date which will not improve customer relations. Better
far to quote terms as 60 days from despatch plus 14 days delivery and
cost the additional period of credit into the price.

Exporters would be wise to quote local discount terms. Two and a
half does not divide happily into decimal currency as the British are

finding out. For this reason the usual Continental terms are 3 per cent 10 days or 2 per cent 30 days or net 60 days. And it should be noted that the Continental customer expects to be able to choose between his 2 per cent discount or his 60 days credit.

In North America there is a phenomenon known as 'anticipation'. If the customer has been quoted, say, net 60-day terms and is feeling relatively flush with money, he may pay 1½ months early and deduct anticipation at 1½ per cent per month – that is, 2¼ per cent on this particular invoice. This applies particularly to textile piece goods. If I. M. Careful Ltd does not wish to allow 'anticipation', his order confirmation should make this clear by saying, for example, 'payment 60 days from despatch plus 15 days in transit strictly net – no anticipation permitted'.

Export collection procedures

Letters of credit, CAD and D/A terms require no additional collection effort on the part of an exporter. There remains the increasingly important area of open account sales. Most of the remarks in Chapter 7 naturally apply but there are a number of additional points worth bearing in mind.

As with domestic trade, if fairly long credit is being granted (90 days upwards) the customer will probably not be surprised if he is asked to accept a bill of exchange. The exporter may wish to discount the bill to finance the credit but even if he does not the bill is a useful collection tool. The invoice should be marked 'Terms – payment by accepted draft at 90 days to be drawn by I. M. Careful Ltd' (or by his local agent perhaps) and the bill sent to the customer at the same time as the goods. The customer will then be able to inspect the goods, accept the bill and return it to I. M. Careful Ltd.

The prevalence of bills varies from country to country. As a generalization, the Latin countries are great users of bills (and takers of credit) while the Scandinavians are the reverse. The exporter can find out the local practice from the foreign department of his bank, the commercial department of the local British embassy, the ECGD, or probably, best of all, from his own sales agent in the country concerned.

Chasing overseas customers for money is a frustrating business. Except with very large amounts the customer will probably pay by airmail transfer. This can take up to two weeks from the date the transfer was authorized to the date it is received and when the post is subject to delay the payment could take up to a month to arrive. One way to improve matters is for I. M. Careful Ltd to open a bank account in, say, Copenhagen for all Danish customers to pay into. Details of payments can be advised daily to the export accounts department of I. M. Careful Ltd. The money could be transferred under standing orders either weekly or whenever the balance exceeds a certain figure by telegraphic transfer.

With difficult collection problems there is one method which is not used in domestic credit. This is the 'demand draft'. I. M. Careful simply draws a bill of exchange payable 'on demand' (see Figure 11:4) for the amount of the overdue account or invoice. It may help if a copy of the statement is attached. He hands this in to his bank with instructions that it be presented for payment at the customer's own bank. When the draft arrives there the bank will request the customer's permission to pay it. If the customer does not instruct the bank to pay, the draft will be returned unpaid. The drawer can give instructions for the bill to be protested if unpaid. The 'demand draft' is an effective inducement because, if it is not paid the customer's bank becomes aware that the customer is under pressure from creditors. This will not necessarily prevent the customer becoming upset at being treated in this way and for this reason the 'demand draft' should be used with discretion.

EXCHANGE FOR Sw. Kr. 25,525   1st January   19 73

At   DEMAND   *pay this* SOLA *Bill of Exchange*
                                                          to the Order of

I.M. CAREFUL LTD, 61 LONDON ROAD, CROYNGE

the sum of Swedish Kroner twenty five thousand five hundred

and twenty five

Value   RECEIVED Invoice 2720 dated   *which place to Account*
. *To*   5th June 1972
          Sven Svenssen AB
          Kastaniealle 19
          Malmegen   for and on behalf of
          6060 Sweden   I. M. CAREFUL LIMITED

Figure 11:4 Bill of exchange payable on demand

Export credit assessment

There are a number of differences between domestic assessment as described in Chapter 6 and export assessment. It is still possible to get an agent's report and of course a reliable agent is a most valuable asset. Trade references are a peculiarly British phenomenon and not much used in certain other countries. Information can be obtained from credit bureaux but this takes longer to obtain than a domestic credit report and foreign reports are up to five times as expensive. Standards vary but in some markets these reports are highly comprehensive. This is particularly true of North America. In many markets the exporter will probably rely largely on a bank reference. He can ask, for example, 'if documentary collections are attended to promptly' if proposing to deal on a CAD basis. As with domestic enquiries, it is well to ask the bank to comment on a figure at the same time stating the proposed terms. Some European bank references are remarkably informative, giving much personal information regarding the owners or managers.

Credit registers are available in certain countries, particularly North America where they are both comprehensive and updated several times a year but they are expensive and only the larger exporters would normally find them worth the cost.

As with domestic credit assessment, perhaps the most reliable guide of all is the exporter's own payments experience. A customer who has always paid promptly is unlikely to prove a bad credit risk. Many exporters use the services of the ECGD which will take over much of the work of credit assessment. However, the individual exporter will have to assess all accounts up to his discretionary limit and may wish occasionally to give credit where he is not covered by his insurer. He would thus be well advised to carry out his own export credit assessment in a methodical and careful manner on those accounts where he is responsible.

Transfer risk

An exporter, in addition to bearing a credit risk, has to consider a transfer risk. He may be dealing with a customer of good standing but who resides in a country which is very short of foreign exchange (in other words the country itself or its currency is the 'credit' risk). Such a country might overnight prohibit payments abroad and in such a case

I. M. Careful's customer cannot obtain sterling or other hard currency with which to discharge his debt. The debt will remain in a bank account temporarily 'blocked'.

What can the UK exporter do about this? First of all he can sell on a *confirmed* letter of credit. If the letter is confirmed by a London bank then that bank is responsible for seeing that the exporter is paid. Alternatively the exporter can insure with the ECGD who will cover 95 per cent of the transfer risk, or he can factor his exports with an export factor who covers 100 per cent of the risk. If he does not wish to insure, the exporter must bear the risk himself and must himself decide which countries are good for their foreign exchange engagements and which are not. The foreign department of his clearing or Scottish bank will be able to advise him.

If he is unfortunate enought to have his export proceeds blocked, he has not necessarily lost them completely. Often this 'blocking' is fairly temporary and amounts to a delay rather than a complete embargo. The local central bank starts rationing its scarce foreign currency and a queue forms. Instead of the foreign currency being available at a day's notice it takes a week, then a month, then perhaps two or three months. On the other hand, the blocking might come as the result of a local revolution in which the new regime declares that, to demonstrate its complete antipathy to the former rulers, their debts will not be honoured: contracts may be unilaterally abrogated by the new regime. In such an atmosphere the actual credit risk increases with the possibility of prominent merchants being liquidated, purged, or stripped of their possessions and it can be seen that the transfer risk and the credit risk are at times closely connected.

Exchange risk

One unit of one currency does not automatically equal so many units of another for more than one day or so at a time. There is no one standard by which other currencies can be measured. Just about all currencies are being bought and sold in terms of other currencies daily on the many foreign-exchange markets of the world. Most monetary authorities aim to maintain a constant value for their currencies in terms of others but relatively few are successful in this aim over long periods although most currencies have until recently been 'pegged' by their managers (a central bank or treasury/finance ministry). Even when pegged, however, they have moved up to 2 per cent either side of the peg. At the time of writing (1973) sterling is not pegged and is officially 'floating' – that is, going up and down daily according to the number of buyers and sellers in the foreign exchange market.

All this poses more problems for the would-be exporter. He can choose whether to invoice in his own currency (sterling) or in the customer's local currency. The first alternative is usually the safest as normally most of an exporter's costs are in sterling and he therefore knows exactly how much sterling his customer will pay him.

However, his customers may not be so anxious to be invoiced in sterling which is to them a foreign currency. The exporter may therefore feel that he would sell more if he invoiced in this customer's own currency. So the exporter has a problem.

The best solution is for the exporter to use the foreign-exchange forward market. As well as buying and selling currencies for immediate (spot) delivery, the foreign-exchange market deals in currencies for forward delivery either on a fixed future date or by giving the other party a limited option over the actual date on which he delivers. No money changes hands when a forward or forward option contract is entered into but each party agrees to buy or sell as the case may be at a rate of exchange which is fixed from the outset. This rate is unlikely to be exactly the same as the spot rate. I. M. Careful Ltd could thus invoice his Swedish customer with Sw.Kr 50,000 goods and at once sell forward the kronor. He might sell the kronor for delivery 30, 60 or 90 days hence or in this case he might well have the contract for delivery 60–90 day option. In this way he insures against a devaluation of the krona by getting a rate at the outset. Provided the customer pays within the 60–90 day period the kronor will merely be applied by his bank against the forward option contract at the rate agreed in the original contract.

If he is dealing regularly with export customers in fairly large amounts and provided the customers pay on a regular basis (this is the value of good credit assessment), I. M. Careful Ltd can take out a series of overlapping forward option contracts, week by week, and the currency proceeds as they come in will be applied against the longest outstanding contract.

Under current Exchange Control Regulations, exporters can cover forward for up to 100 per cent of their firm commitments in foreign exchange and they are not permitted to cover more than 100 per cent. Bearing in mind the normal incidence of credit notes, settlement discounts, disputes, counterclaims and any other elements inherent in a sale which, in the end, are not going to be paid by the customer, it is perhaps prudent to estimate these in total as a percentage of sales and deduct this from the 100 per cent cover. For example, if I. M. Careful Ltd estimates that he only receives settlement of 93 per cent of his export invoices he is well advised to enter into forward foreign-exchange contracts covering about 93 per cent of his sales. Such a scheme gives almost complete cover against foreign-currency devaluations and once set up is relatively simple to operate.

Currency	Spot rate	3 months forward premium	
		amount	per cent
US dollar	2.3465	1.95¢ pm	0.8%
Canadian dollar	2.3375	2.13¢ pm	0.9%
Dutch gulden	7.56	8¾c pm	1.15%
Belgian franc	103.25	85c pm	0.8%
Danish krone	16.04	7 øre dis	(0.4%) discount
Deutschmark	7.50	10 pfg pm	1.3%
Portuguese escudo	62.70	40 c pm	0.75%
Italian lira	1,365.00	2½ lire dis	(0.2%) discount
Norwegian krone	15.56	10 øre pm	0.6%
French franc	12.00	3½ c pm	0.3%
Swedish krona	11.11½	9 öre pm	0.8%
Austrian schilling	54.15	45 groschen pm	0.8%
Swiss franc	8.83½	8¾ c pm	1.0%

Figure 11:5 Closing rates for foreign currencies on 2 January 1973

This is not the only attraction. The British exporter at least will get his foreign-exchange cover not only virtually free but usually with a cash bonus thrown in. This is because historically most currencies have been at a forward premium against sterling during most of the postwar era. (This is due to a variety of technical reasons and is only partly a reflection of the floating pound.) The table in Figure 11:5 shows the closing rates for various foreign currencies on 2 January 1973.

Out of these 13 most important world currencies, two are at a discount in the forward market and the remainder are at a premium. The profit which I. M. Careful would make on the forward sales of the proceeds of his Sw.Kr 50,000 invoice would amount to just Kr 400 or, in sterling terms, a profit of £36 on a sale of £4,505. Not very much perhaps but this premium is available on the majority of export sales and it is well worth taking a little trouble to secure. Exactly how much profit I. M. Careful would make using the forward market in this way would depend on the markets or currencies in which he was selling.

CHAPTER 12

The Computer as an Aid to Credit Management

This chapter does not seek to instruct the reader on how to program a computer or even on how to run a computerized accounting system. We hope the chapter will be of help to the financial director or credit manager of a company which is proposing to computerize and that it will have a few ideas to help those who have already gone through this sometimes traumatic experience.

What is a computer?

What is a computer? Essentially it is a machine with a very large capacity for sorting and storing data, or transactions, and with the ability to compare data against whatever parameters are fed into it. The computer itself works unbelievably fast but there are two bottlenecks in every computer system: putting in the information and getting it out again. The input of data is where most of the difficulties arise. The transactions – for example invoices for customers' accounts or cash from customers' payments – have to be converted from the normal written form to something the computer can assimilate. This is usually in the form of punched cards, punched paper tape or magnetic tape.

The information on the invoice has to be 'coded' — that is, converted into a series of holes or degrees of magnetization which the computer can read. Almost invariably the computer will identify a customer not by his name but by the account number which he has been allotted. The function of coding invoices and other transactions is thus very important and the coded data must be carefully checked and double checked, otherwise errors will creep in and problems will result.

The extraction of information is a mechanical rather than a management problem. Even with printers capable of 1200 lines per minute it takes a relatively long time to print out a complete sales ledger or the customers' statements. A computer is a very exact instrument. If incorrect data are fed into it, it will continue to perpetuate the error until someone goes to the trouble of correcting it. Conversely if the right information is fed in the right answer comes out. Preparation of data is thus all important.

Running a sales accounting system successfully demands a new degree of discipline because, whereas a company can muddle along in the traditional manual system relying on a blitz every six months or so to keep things reasonably straight, it is impossible to muddle along with a computer — the situation would rapidly develop into a nightmare. Having acquired the necessary disciplines the computerized system becomes in fact much easier to run than most manual systems and the business of trial balances and preparation of monthly accounts becomes an automatic routine — no more the midnight oil and endless delays tracking down the double entry that was only half completed, for every computer debit will automatically produce a corresponding credit.

Having grasped this last point firmly, some companies have made the unhappy choice of installing a computer in place of a messy manual system without first getting the input right. Their computer starts its life at a hopeless disadvantage under those conditions. It follows that an ill-disciplined accounts department must first put its house in order before going live on a computer and, to make quite sure — even in the best regulated families — it is wise to run the manual and computer systems in tandem for a couple of months, if for no other reason than to inspire the confidence of the staff in the new system.

Control section

The flow diagram in Figure 12.1 shows the relationship between the computer and different aspects of the sales ledger operation. It will be

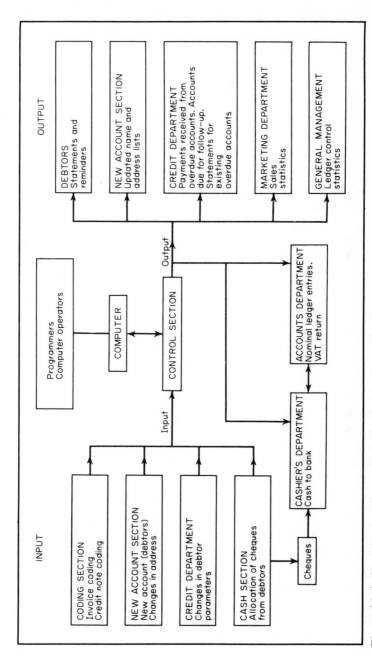

Figure 12:1 Organization chart of computerized sales-ledger function

165

seen that the 'control section' is the hub of the operation. It receives the prepared input data, notes the total figures for debits and credits and passes the data forward to the computer. Once the computer has completed its run the results return to the control section which compares the output totals to those of the input and *identifies and lists the differences.* This is all important.

However carefully data is prepared, mistakes are bound to occur. For example, an invoice may have been coded for a new account but the new account has not been set up on the computer files. The computer will reject the invoice. The job of the control section is to identify the invoice concerned, find out why the account has not been set up, have it set up and resubmit the invoice for computer processing. Until such time as the invoice is resubmitted it must be held on a suspense account. Obviously the more errors which occur the more difficult the work of the control section. But errors cannot be eliminated and therefore must be strictly controlled and accounted for.

A typical control section's sales-ledger reconciliation might look like the one in Figure 12.2. As soon as the computer completes the day's processing a new update figure will become available incorporating today's invoices, credit notes and cash and (probably) a new error report will have to be inserted. If more than three days' error reports are outstanding at once then something would appear to be seriously wrong and the data processing manager should investigate at once.

The second responsibility of the control section is to ensure that data are received from the user department in good time for the update processing as laid down by the data preparation manager. The third function of the section is to check that all the scheduled update processing has in fact been completed and to distribute the results of this updating process to interested departments.

Sales ledger as per last update		£729,245.70
Add/deduct error report 27	£27,129.50 DR	
Add/deduct error report 29	5,013.22 CR	
Add today's new invoices	64,257.17 DR	
Deduct today's new credit notes	329.20 CR	
Deduct today's new cash/discount	48,300.16 CR	
Add/deduct today's journals	—	
Adjusted sales-ledger balance as at today		£766,989.79

Figure 12:2 Sales-ledger reconciliation

It is important to note that accurate data preparation coupled with an efficient control section will not eliminate all sales-ledger difficulties: there remains the important task of reconciliation and agreement with customers of their balances and there is also the problem with an open-item computerized ledger of 'on-account' or unapplied cash. The first of these is not confined to computerized sales ledgers alone and the second is discussed later in this chapter.

Choice of machine

Successful installation of a computer calls for a clear understanding of the roles which different parties must play in this achievement. First there is the computer company which may advise the purchase or leasing of an unnecessarily large or expensive machine. For example, disks are more expensive than tapes but they afford the advantage of random access, which means items of data scattered through long records can be more quickly extracted. However, it does not follow that everyone needs the more expensive disk system if the cheaper tape system produces the user's requirements in reasonable time.

Most companies that have to tackle this question for the first time will not have sufficient technical knowledge to weigh the relative merits of size, scope and speed in relation to their requirements and the price of a given computer system. A computer manufacturer can hardly be expected to be objective on the question of which machine to buy but once this is decided the manufacturer can provide considerable technical help. Neither a consultant nor the experts in a computer-manufacturing company are really in a position to define management's specific requirements for their computer. This is the job of the user's line management.

As a first step, line management must consider and list every requirement stating both layout and frequency. These requirements should be divided into essential, useful and peripheral. The adviser or systems analyst can, with the help of the computer company or on his own, estimate the computer capacity required and the most appropriate system. Before the final decision on specification is reached, it will become clear that the cost of producing some of the peripheral information is greater than its value and if requirements are confined to the essential output and some of the useful information then a much cheaper computer configuration might be employed with advantage.

The outline plan having been evolved, line management must estimate its growth requirements over at least the next five years and at the same time study ways and means of developing peripheral information at little or no extra computer cost.

Assuming line management is now satisfied that they have thought of everything they require and the computer adviser is satisfied that the configuration will meet these requirements in terms of both quantity and frequency, the user is now ready to place his order for the computer and, with his advisers, must evolve a complicated timetable covering training of programmers, machine operators and sales accounting staff who will have to prepare the 'input' when the computer goes live. Special continuous stationery not only has to be ordered but also probably designed and this will involve a joint effort between line management who require something easily understood and the computer experts who know better how this can be produced most quickly and therefore cheaply. The time scale during the preparation period is vital: if it is too short the objective will not be met and if it is too long impetus and enthusiasm will be lost, not to mention the risk of wasted assets.

Credit department and the computer

The credit department's first concern is not with the coding of invoices: perhaps the most important information to them is the names and addresses of customers. It has already been pointed out that every customer has to have a number. Since the credit department maintain the records of customers' creditworthiness they would be well advised to look after the register of names and numbers to ensure that they are both accurate and up to date. In a manual system, all that is necessary to do on a group account is to write in pencil on the card 'Care – part of XYZ Group – send statement to . . . . '. In a computerized system the name and address must be properly amended – this takes extra time at the outset but thereafter the account will run more smoothly. So a significant part of the cost of computerizing will be the setting up of a name and address section, or the appointment of a clerk with responsibility for this aspect.

One of the first points which the credit department should consider is what items of information on each customer's account they are interested in. The name, address and account number have already been seen to be necessary but in addition it is feasible to show other information: the credit rating, the internal refer limit, the discretionary amount which the sales office may despatch without reference to the credit department. It might also be worth recording the precise cash discount terms appropriate to each account. All this increases the work of setting up the ledger but once this information is *accurately* shown on every account it is an aid to the efficient running of the ledger. Not all this information should of course feature on the statement which is sent to the customer but it should be available on an internal ledger or credit report.

Further information of interest to the credit department can be added automatically to each account record by the computer, for example:

1 Highest debit balance, this year, last year and the year before.
2 Highest single payment received, this year, last year and the year before.
3 Date of last cash receipt.
4 Monthly turnover for last 12 months (or longer).
5 Breakdown by age of invoice (not due, 1-30 days overdue, 31-60 days overdue, etc.).
6 Number of reminder letters sent.

This information requires no clerical effort on the part of the credit or accounts department but merely some forethought. This is because the computer can be programmed to retain this information while the system is being set up but it is most unlikely that existing programs can be adapted to take them once the system is complete – unlikely, that is, without a massive revision of the system.

The value of this additional information is that it gives to the credit department most of the information they would obtain from an examination of the conventional ledger card.

The computer should not merely be a creator of more work, it will itself do some of the former manual work of the credit department if sensibly programmed to do so. One of the most obvious chores which can be given to the machine is the preparation of routine reminder letters to overdue accounts. These can be controlled by means of the parameters discussed above.

More than one series of reminder messages is possible to 'personalize' the approach. There is little point in listing the reminders first, second,

Age of oldest item past due date	Message
14–28 days	As this account is now due please forward your payment if this is not already in the post.
29–42 days	Your payment of this account now will obviate further reminders and oblige.
43–56 days	We still have not received your payment or reason for withholding it. Please remit.
57–70 days	This account is now overdue. Please remit at once.
71 days and over	Despite many reminders this account is still unpaid. Kindly forward your payment today.

Figure 12:3 Computer reminder messages

third, etc., and it is a better plan to arrange to mix the different series in a random way so that the debtor cannot work out for himself how close he is to having his supplies cut off and sterner action taken.

The reminder should be brief but not unduly so. A series of reminders suitable for a computer is shown in Figure 12.3. Two points must be noted: first of all a reminder could be sent automatically to a credit balance if this comprised a small overdue invoice and a larger credit note. Credit balances must either be programmed out of the reminder system or removed manually from the post tray. Second, the computer cannot be responsible for the whole collection effort and it is for this reason that in Figure 12.3 there are no messages for accounts over 90 days overdue. These customers must be considered on their merits by a human and not an electronic brain.

Open-Item System

The usual manual sales ledger works on the basis of a brought-forward balance from last month and itemized transactions for the current month. Sometimes several months' transactions are shown on the statement but there is still a brought-forward balance at the top of the page. It is possible to have a system with brought-forward balances on a computer, but it is not normally practical to show more than one month in detail. This is not the best system on a computer because it makes detailed ageing of the ledger impossible and is clumsy as it requires constant reference back to different earlier months' statements. Instead most computers use the open-item system or a modification of it. Under this system all unpaid invoices are shown but once an invoice is paid it is removed together with the payment.

Day 1

Invoice/Credit Note Number	Date	Debit	Credit	Balance
1012	21.1.73	62.50		
1013	21.1.73	91.25		
1180	12.2.73	275.00		
817	13.3.73		10.00	418.75

Day 2 after payment of £143.75

1180	12.2.73	275.00		275.00

Figure 12:4 Operation of the open-item system

For example, in Figure 12.4 the cheque has been credited to the account and the two earliest invoices and the credit note removed leaving just invoice 1180 still owing.

The great advantage of this method is that each account can be broken down into:

1   Not yet due.
2   0-30 days overdue.
3   31-60 days overdue.
4   61-90 days overdue.
5   Over 90 days overdue.
6   Unapplied credits.
7   Total.

Moreover, the total ledger can be broken down in this way so that the credit manager and financial director can easily see if the overdue position is getting better or worse. The disadvantage from the credit controller's point of view is that he loses the historical detail on the ledger card which shows him exactly how the account has been conducted.

Our experience is that recording both the highest balance and highest payment in each of the last three years coupled with monthly turnover for the last 12 months gives enough information to make accurate credit judgments.

It would be foolish to suppose that this system consists entirely of advantages and is devoid of disadvantages. The open-item system is cumbersome where a significant proportion of the customers make round-sum payments on account or short payments without giving any adequate reason or when they fail to pay to an exact balance. A payment which does not match a debit or a collection of debits has to show as a credit on the account and this gives rise to 'unapplied cash'. If this unapplied element builds up, the age-of-debts analysis becomes distorted in so far as old debts are recorded in total but there are unidentified credits to match a proportion of them.

This problem cannot be entirely eliminated and special efforts have to be made to reconcile accounts periodically which have an accumulation of unapplied cash. This, of course, requires the cooperation of the customer whose own accounting system may be less well disciplined and those customers who are accustomed to making round-sum payments must be invited from time to time to 'pay to an agreed balance'. This having been done, the slate can be wiped clean up to that point thus releasing computer space for current transactions.

The same argument applies to credit notes as to cash. When a credit is claimed it frequently relates to part of an invoice rather than an entire invoice. In these cases it will not obviously match a debit already in the records. It follows that a credit note, which normally bears a separate number series from the invoice series, should also show the invoice number to which it relates. The unpaid balance of any particular invoice can thus be easily identified and, if remaining unpaid, can be specifically noted on the computer record.

These disadvantages are relatively minor when compared with the benefits of both detailed and overall control which the computer provides to the credit department. For management control, monthly or weekly, even daily returns of overdue accounts can be produced simply and quickly. Indeed the computer is quite capable of generating so much control information that management becomes inundated with paper which the mind fails to assimilate.

Here again line management must think through most carefully just what control information they require to enable them to see the wood for the trees so that important information is not scattered through a mass of unimportant information and thereby at risk of being missed. The shorter the control reports the better, for they will then highlight the major areas of concern to management and at the same time reduce the computer running costs.

CHAPTER 13

The Credit Function

If the credit function is to be effective it must not only be organized within itself but, even more important, its precise powers must be clearly defined in relation to other aspects of the whole business. Perhaps the first essential is to establish the 'balance of power' between sales and credit. If there is an imbalance in favour of sales then the credit function will not operate effectively because those employed on the credit side will grow frustrated through constant overruling and they will gradually stop trying to do their job properly. If there is an imbalance in favour of credit the same repercussions may affect the sales effort. This is less likely because most firms employ a senior person or director as head of sales whereas they usually employ a less important person on the credit side. Indeed the credit function is frequently the part-time responsibility of the accountant or even the secretary. Sales, however, is usually a full-time job and in this type of situation the sales considerations will tend to overrule the credit considerations. Such an arrangement is good when:

1 All sales are for cash; or
2 All sales are made to absolutely undoubted customers; or
3 The gross margin of profit on each article sold is so great that a high percentage of bad debts can be profitably sustained.

174

In these circumstances there is little point in having a credit side to the business at all. If, as is more common, trading circumstances involve both smaller margins and the granting of credit to customers who are not undoubted, then it is wrong if sales dictate to credit.

Establishing a credit policy for a company

Whether the credit function is a part-time job for one man or the work of a department, the terms of reference for the one man or the head of the department should be clearly laid down and a written statement of company policy regarding credit should be issued. This might include directives on the following points:

1   The tolerance level of bad debts expressed perhaps as a percentage of sales turnover.
2   The normal trade terms and what powers, if any, the credit manager has to vary the norm.
3   The amount up to which he may approve credit without reference to higher authority.
4   His precise powers to stop further deliveries to bad risks or deteriorating accounts and how these powers are to be exercised.
5   How much research he is to make before approving credit and, against this, how quickly is he expected to make his decisions. A lot of research and high speed are incompatible; which is more important? This will vary from one business to another.
6   To whom should his decisions or advice be communicated and, in the event of disagreement, who will be the arbiter?
7   Concerning the collection of overdue accounts, the tone and frequency of approach to customers should be established together with guidance on where exceptions to the normal procedure are justified. For instance, it would be foolish to send a long telegram for a 50p debt but it might be wise to make a long-distance phone call to a fairly new customer owing £2,000 when the account is ten days overdue.
8   At what stage should an account be passed to solicitors for legal action and what other steps have to be taken internally before such action is taken.

A few hours' careful thought and a discussion with the credit manager will probably be quite sufficient to prepare a written brief on the company's credit policy. This policy must, of course, also have been agreed with the sales department beforehand. If this brief is then issued to all heads of departments they will all know what the policy is and what the credit manager's brief is. Provided he sticks to it there will be little room for interdepartmental recrimination – an all too frequent occurrence in unsatisfactory relationships between credit and sales.

Careful wording is necessary. If the brief to sales is 'maximum sales' and the brief to credit is 'no bad debts', conflict and wasted energy are almost inevitable. If the brief to both is 'maximum profit achieved by maximum sales to sound customers coupled with a reasonable minimum of bad debts' then maximum profit is more likely to follow coupled with a harmonious as opposed to a discordant sales-credit relationship.

Responsibility for the credit function

In a company where the credit function is not a full-time job for a senior man but is nevertheless important, the commonest mistake is to pass this function to the accountant who is more often than not too involved with other important priorities to give credit the attention it deserves. To keep books of account, to prepare balance sheets, to cost, to produce budgets, to control wages and other company expenditure are all functions pertaining to the accountant yet they have nothing to do with the credit function. It is primarily because the accountant is responsible for all the many aspects of 'making both ends meet' that he has insufficient time left to devote to credit. If he does devote time to credit one of his other important functions may suffer. It is best, therefore, to find an employee with intelligence and ambition (and a rudimentary knowledge of book-keeping) who can be told that the credit question is his number-one priority. It can, therefore, be a part-time job but it must come first for the person selected.

The credit manager needs to be both perceptive and resilient. He must be able to stand up to pressure from within and without. He must have the ability to make reasoned sensible decisions and to defend those decisions intelligently when they are questioned. He will, therefore, usually be either a young man with drive and intelligence who is clearly on the promotion ladder or an older man with a deal of experience in business and human relationships.

The credit manager should be answerable to the managing director, preferably directly but otherwise through the secretary or lastly the accountant. He should never be answerable to either the sales or the production departments where he may be subject to pressures which can distort objective judgment. The credit manager must be given powers to decide credit questions or to advise senior management upon them. There is no point in employing a man to advise if his advice is rarely taken. Only the managing director should be able to overrule the credit manager, and he should rarely do so. If it is necessary to overrule the credit manager frequently, his advice or decisions are of little value to the company and he should not be employed in that role.

A credit communications network

Perhaps the most vital factor in achieving efficient credit management is the establishment of good communications between the various departments. Many people think of credit as a sort of guessing game; they think of a good credit manager as one possessing a mystique or some kind of extra-sensory perception not given to ordinary mortals. There are those who cultivate this concept. In point of fact this is just so much mumbo-jumbo.

The good credit manager is the man who collects all relevant information, weighs it, stores it, and acts upon it. If follows from this that it is useful to have a good memory but the value of this asset is by no means confined to credit managers. Perhaps even more important is a good filing system. But most important of all is the speedy feedback of accurate information. It is accurate information that reduces the element of luck, which must always be inherent in questions of credit, to a tolerable minimum. There is always an 'unknown quantity' in credit. The aim must be to reduce that unknown quantity to a minimum. For example, the good credit manager may have, say, eight positive pieces of information of which five are favourable, one unfavourable and two in the balance. He may also know that there are two other important factors unknown to him and about which he cannot find out. In making his decision he has, however, weighed 80 per cent of the factors and he can make some allowance for the 20 per cent unknown. He has thus reduced the 'luck factor' by four-fifths. This is the good credit manager's real mystique – the reduction of the luck factor to a tolerable minimum. It is axiomatic that too many bad debts reflect bad judgment but good judgment cannot be made without accurate information. Conversely, too few bad debts may also reflect bad judgment if sales and profits are heavily curtailed because the company attempts to eliminate bad debts altogether. Thus a highly efficient system of communications is the first essential in maintaining an effective but flexible control over credit.

Lines of communication

Figure 13.1 shows the lines of direct communication which should be established and maintained between operational functions or departments. The company secretary has been omitted not because he has been forgotten but because he is something of a specialist whose duties span many aspects, especially if personnel management lies within his orbit. The purpose of this diagram is to demonstrate exactly how the credit lines of communication fit within the general communication structure of a company. Clearly some companies will require departments and communications which are not depicted here but the majority of firms will find it desirable to establish and maintain the lines which are shown in addition to their other more specialized requirements.

In smaller companies some of the functions may be combined within one department or may be carried out by one individual. This does not alter the principle in any way. If these lines are not both established and maintained, frustration, delay, and inefficiency are likely to result. For instance, if the credit function is subjugated to the sales-ledger function and is thereby forced to communicate with the rest of the company through the accountant, it is probable that a bottleneck will result in the accounts function. By arranging direct lines this type of difficulty is avoided and key management is freed from handling routine detail which can more effectively be dealt with on a direct net.

Of course adequate arrangements must be made to keep central management informed of decisions and actions taken, perhaps by a system of 'information copies'. Information copies will normally pass along the lines drawn on the diagram.

Figure 13.2 depicts the sequence of events after a customer has placed an order. In the case of a new customer, trade references may be required and sufficient time allowed for making further inquiries and setting up the control features in both the sales ledgers and despatch departments. In the case of an old customer the process should and

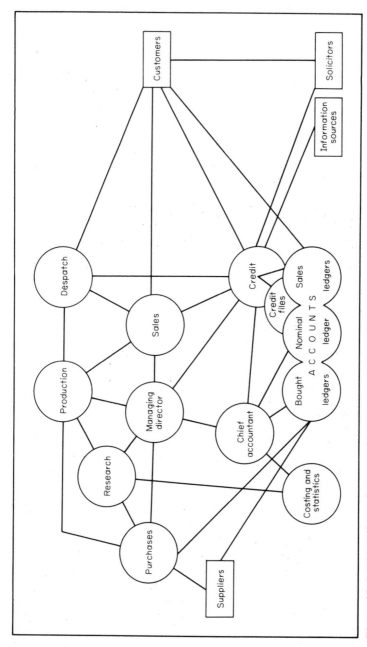

Figure 13:1 Direct lines of communication

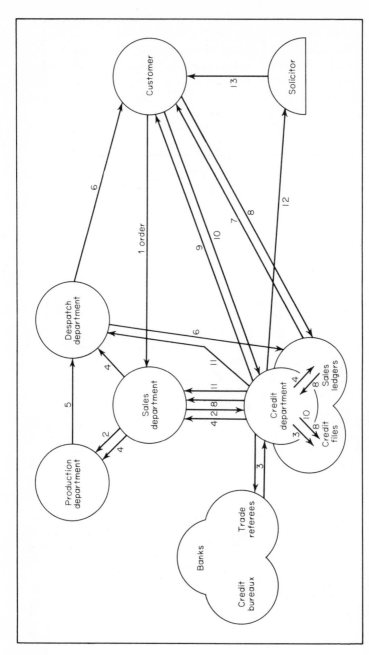

Figure 13:2 Sequence of action from receipt of a customer's order
The numbers on this diagram are explained on page 181

must be much quicker as it will not normally be necessary to inquire outside the company. However, the diagram shows the sequence of events through to a legal action if this is necessary, although stage 8 will more usually be the last process. From this diagram the need for direct communications between departments can be apreciated. Figure 13.1 depicts the lines of communication which should be established and maintained for both action and information purposes.

Credit-sales liaison

This is perhaps the most important link in the chain but it is here that rivalry or conflict is most likely to arise unless care is taken by

---

Figure 13.2 shows

1 Sales obtain order (and trade references) from customer.
2 Sales inform credit and production (warning order).
3 Credit checks own files and obtains information as necessary from third parties.
4 Credit informs sales of approval or otherwise of order and any standing arrangements for credit (shipping codes, etc). This information is passed on to production and despatch. Credit establishes appropriate controls in sales ledgers.
5 Production is completed and goods passed to despatch.
6 Despatch send goods to customer and copy of documentation (delivery note or invoice) to sales ledgers.
7 Sales ledgers record transaction (prepare final invoice) and send statement to customer.
8 Customer settles his account or queries it or does not reply to routine reminders. Sales ledgers inform credit of this. Credit passes queries to sales for investigation.
9 If no reply from customer, credit writes special letter to customer or telephones.
10 Customer responds or does not respond.
11 If no response, credit informs despatch (copy to sales) to cancel discretionary shipping code and refer all transactions to credit. Sales may seek alternative customers for goods already in production.
12 If still no response from customer to a final reminder, credit passes account to solicitor for legal action.
13 Unlucky for some. A writ or other appropriate legal action (see Chapter 7).

management to ensure it does not. There is a job of image building to be done here because it is quite normal for salesmen to know little about credit and credit managers to know little about selling. They should be brought together to attend lectures on the importance of each. The credit manager should, for instance, be invited to attend the sales director's conference or training session with the representatives. This should be of mutual benefit and should serve to break down the sales misconception that credit men are merely obstructive and the credit manager's misconception that salesmen lack intelligence.

Representatives should also be encouraged to spend a day with the credit manager since even a cursory view of the credit administration will greatly help to speed up communications between the two functions and help to establish a satisfactory mutual understanding.

Of course the keen young salesman will naturally be upset if an attractive order he has obtained is declined on credit grounds. Credit managers would do well to realize themselves that this is a natural reaction and they must take active steps to see that the credit department's reputation with the sales force is high. This can be done in only one way: by adopting a positive approach to all credit-sales problems.

There are few customers so bad that they merit no credit at all.

There are few that are so good that their credit should be 'un-limited' – a dangerous word in credit work because it is imprecise and therefore conveys different meanings to different people. It is therefore almost always a question of how much credit rather than of 'yes' or 'no'. The credit department's image will inevitably be damaged if the answer to a proposal is a simple 'no' (except in those few cases where it is right that absolutely no credit should be granted) yet many credit managers when faced with an overlarge order will say just that. This is the negative approach.

The positive approach is to seek out and find a prudent way of effecting the desired transaction. This involves some extra work and effort all round and, incidentally, this is another reason why this function should not be delegated to someone with more pressing priorities or someone lacking initiative. The credit manager should first explore the practical possibility of 'splitting the delivery'. Hence he may find an ally in the production department whom it may suit to arrange delivery in two parts. It might also suit the customer or at least not inconvenience him. Splitting the delivery will help to spread the credit risk by enabling delivery of the second part to be made after payment of the first part.

Again, the question of shorter credit terms might be considered, thus reducing the time risk when it is impossible to reduce the amount risk. Such a suggestion might be sweetened for the customer by offering an attractive cash discount for prompt payment. Alternatively, it might be suggested that the customer pays 25 per cent of the value with the order and/or 25 per cent on delivery or even 50 per cent with order. If the customer really requires the goods urgently he may be quite glad to receive 50 per cent credit in exchange for 50 per cent cash. It may be that all these suggestions fall on deaf ears but at least no one can say the credit manager did not try to find a way to facilitate trade on a sound basis and on the occasions when this approach succeeds all parties will be appreciative.

The credit manager's positive contribution to the sales effort does not end here. He should get to know his ledger and grade his customers in order of size and behaviour. He may find it convenient to establish amounts which can prudently be despatched without prior reference to himself. This list should be provided to the despatch manager to save unnecessary checking with the credit department. Such a list is, or should be, of great value to the sales force as they can see from it exactly to what extent each customer enjoys the confidence of the credit department.

With this information the sales department can devote time proportionately to the quality of the customer, spending most time on the best and avoiding altogether the worst. Indeed, it should be possible for the informed credit manager to fit every account appropriately into one of the 25 squares shown in Figure 13.3. Customers can then be graded, for example, from A1 to E5. The shaded area of the table indicates the danger area which most firms should try to avoid when granting credit. This information is of course of a highly confidential nature and this should be clearly understood by the sales force.

Credit-despatch liaison

As mentioned earlier, the credit manager should be vested with the power to stop deliveries to deteriorating accounts. Without these powers he will be unable to effect the control outlined in Chapter 6. He must, therefore, have communications with the despatch department

Size of business	Payments performance				
	1 Prompt	2 Normal	3 Slow	4 Very slow	5 Bad risk
A Very large					
B Large					
C Medium					
D Small					
E One man					

Figure 13:3 Payments grading

but he must at the same time keep the sales department informed. A salesman, unbeknown to him, may be in the area at that very moment and a man on the spot may be able to investigate and sometimes solve the problem outright, thus restoring confidence all round quickly. It is fairly common practice to circulate the 'overdue list' but this should not necessarily mean the same thing as the 'stop list' or the 'refer list'.

Stopping deliveries. It is not necessarily prudent or wise to stop deliveries to all companies just because their accounts happen to be overdue; before such a decision is taken the credit manager should be satisfied that there is no valid reason why an account remains unpaid. It follows that, quite apart from communicating with the customer to find out why his account has not been paid, the sales or production or accounts departments, or anyone else in the firm who learns of a customer's complaint, should route it to the credit manager so that he may appropriately adjust his thinking on the credit aspect and make due allowance for this irregularity before stopping despatch.

Assuming that there is no valid reason for non-payment, the credit manager should stop further deliveries 'pending settlement of the overdue account'. This is important. It will make the customer, who put all the earlier reminders in the wastepaper basket, sit up. He may even draw a cheque as he muses over this unusual treatment. This is much cheaper than employing a solicitor and sometimes more effective too.

Restarting stopped credit. Almost more important than stopping deliveries is the question of restarting them. For this reason it is vital that the credit manager is immediately informed by the accounts department (sales ledgers) that payment has been received on a stopped account. Depending upon the adquacy of the payment and the size of the remaining balance, the credit manager will then tell the despatch department that goods may go or he may decide to approach the customer for a further payment. Again sales must know of this fresh development and speed of communication is vital to retain the goodwill of customers.

Techniques to speed the exchange of information

The aim must be to arrange communications in such a way that the lines are not clogged with routine or non-urgent information and are thus left free for urgent communications. Certain types of information should be exchanged on lists in writing. Information should be passed only to those who need to know. The sales department needs to know about the customers it is either approaching or being approached by. They do not need information about customers with whom they have ceased to do business. The accounts department needs to know which customers it is required to report on. It does not need to know the precise situation in the production or despatch departments at any given moment.

It will be seen from this that an effective credit manager should be the nerve centre of the business so far as information about customers is concerned and he will find that a good filing system ready to hand is a vital tool of his trade. Here can be stored the history of events which build the complete credit picture and here also can be stored that useful information which is not, for the moment, required.

Shipping codes. It is a bad thing to give the sales force a list of customers' credit limits. Such a list is liable to give rise to misunderstandings and embarrassments. Customers do not stand still and their financial strength is changing continuously. If salesmen were to be provided with credit limits for each customer they would be faced with just two unsatisfactory alternatives: either they will be bombarded with amendments to such an extent that this will hamper the sales effort or their lists will become out of date and inaccurate with the passage of time.

A better way of overcoming this difficulty is to allocate a 'shipping code' to each customer. This code can be expressed in the value of despatches each day, week, or month according to the delivery pattern of the trade. For example, if customer A is considered good for £1,500 total credit at any one time, but he normally buys between £150 and £250 every week, his account could with safety be given a shipping code of £250 a week. This information would be passed to both sales and despatch departments as a standing arrangement for customer A. The effect of this is to cut out unnecessary communications. Customer A's account rolls on unhampered so long as it remains in its normal state.

If the customer's payments slow up then the matter will be referred by sales ledgers to credit because of the controls which have been set up in the sales ledger by the credit manager as described in Chapter 6. If the size of orders increases above the shipping code they will have to be referred specifically to credit for sanction. By the time either of these changes in trading pattern occurs, it may be appropriate to reconsider the shipping code and/or the control figure in sales ledgers.

By operating liaison in this way, communications between the various departments are confined to matters of moment and only those customers' accounts which *need* to be reviewed up or down are reconsidered and assessed. There is really no need to review the accounts which are operating satisfactorily and within their credit assessment figure. By being selective in this way, it may be possible to control up to 90 per cent of all transactions on a routine basis. Thus the credit manager can concentrate on the 10 per cent or so exceptions where he is of most value. The exceptions are, on the one side, the seriously overdue accounts which need special care and maintenance and, on the other side, those on which exceptionally large orders arise. Exceptionally large orders are defined by reference to the shipping code.

The establishment of a shipping code for each customer involves several hours' work. A good credit manager will do well to fix 500 or so in a day. The establishment of these codes should be a joint operation with the sales director. Sales and credit should therefore sit down together to measure the sales requirement of each customer in relation to the credit assessment. The majority of cases will present little difficulty provided both parties are reasonable because most customers in any case keep their normal requirements within their own capacity to meet their obligations. In the cases where the sales department requires more credit to be given than the credit manager deems prudent, more detailed information should be obtained with a view to increasing the credit assessment or spreading the delivery programme, or changing the payments terms. Once this job has been done, a basis of understanding has been established between the credit and sales departments which is of immense value to both and will enable them to cooperate effectively when questions of reviews and increases arise later. Moreover, once done, the job does not have to be done again, as changes need only occur in the light of the practical requirements as they arise.

Refer-all-transactions lists. Almost inevitably amongst customers there will be those whose affairs are not prospering as they would wish. The first sign of this to the outsider is usually a deterioration in the payments performance. In such a situation it may be necessary to suspend, at least temporarily, the shipping code arrangements established with the sales and despatch departments until such time as the position is redressed. A stop list is a credit weapon which, like the credit limit, leads again to misunderstanding and embarrassment with customers. The purpose of the 'refer-all-transactions list' is similar to that of the stop list but it is a more flexible tool yet no less effective because, instead of stopping deliveries, its effect is to withdraw the shipping code and make all deliveries depend on *prior reference* to the credit manager. The advantages are as follows: the credit manager becomes aware that further despatches are ready and he can use this knowledge to induce payment of an amount past due. Instead of someone saying to a customer: 'You cannot have the goods you want because you are on the stop list' – an all too frequent remark – the credit manager can telephone the customer and say, 'The payment of your account will enable us to expedite delivery of your next order which we are pleased to have received.' This usually works wonders whereas the other approach is more likely to engender annoyance and even guilt complexes.

There is yet another psychological reason for operating the refer list arrangement between the sales, despatch, and credit departments. If a delivery of further goods which the customer requires will be expedited by his payment, the customer has something positive to gain from paying this particular account now as opposed to some other supplier's account. He is also more likely to develop a healthy repect for this particular supplier's administration and he may make a note that this account is one which should be paid promptly because it is obviously watched. If, on the other hand, goods are delivered without reference to the state of an already overdue account, the cusotmer will have obtained his immediate requirements without having to have made a payment and there is thereafter no immediate inducement for him to pay. He may even go so far as to make a mental note that this account is one he can take his time over paying and thus other creditors who are more persistent will be preferred. Many firms have only a limited amount of cash available to meet their current commitments and there is just not enough cash to meet them all as they fall due. Creditors are, therefore, to some extent competing with one another for settlement of their accounts. It follows from this that the creditor or supplier with the most efficient system of control and collection will be the one who is paid first. The savings which flow from this are not only the reduction of the bad-debt risk and hence the reduction of actual bad debts. There is an incalculable saving on: (a) interest on financing debtor balances, (b) letter writing, (c) filing and recording, and (d) communications between departments. In short, time and money are saved all round.

CHAPTER 14

Organization of a Credit Department

Whereas up to this point the credit function has been considered as though it were the job of one man or even, in smaller organizations, the part-time job of one man, it will be found economical in larger organizations to delegate within this area so that the most able person in credit management can be released from the more routine duties and concentrate on the most difficult credit problems. The whole question of credit involves the selection of priorities and the man in charge must have both the power and the ability to do this. Let us call him the credit manager.

The organization of a credit department will depend to a large extent on the nature of the company's business. To give two extreme opposite examples: one company may have 300 customers with many credit risks in the £5,000 to £100,000 bracket; another company may have 10,000 accounts of which most are in the £50 to £1,000 bracket. The first company will obviously require a different type of manager from the second. The first requires an able man with perhaps a junior. The second will require many more juniors and the manager will require more organizing ability though possibly rather less financial acumen.

As soon as there is more credit work than he can efficiently cope with the credit manager will require an assistant. This type of work cannot be learned in a couple of weeks. Assuming the right man has been selected it will take about six months' training before he can reasonably be expected to start taking minor credit decisions on his own. Therefore, if a company is growing, the acquisistion and training of credit personnel must be planned well in advance of the requirement.

A good credit man in a well organized department will be able to control and handle two or three times as much work after eighteen months or so, as he could after six months. A balance has to be found in acquiring staff in relation to the anticipated growth of the company. Because it takes a relatively long time to train a credit assistant, careful selection in the first place is important because if the wrong man is selected it can set the department back by six months to a year.

Functions which can be delegated

Much of the work which has to be done in a credit department lends itself to routine procedures. At the same time special urgent situations, for which there may be no readily available precedent, will arise from time to time without prior warning. Routines should therefore be established but they must be flexible so that if the need arises they can be temporarily suspended and then reinstated with the minimum of trouble once the crisis hss been dealt with. The art of delegation is to distinguish between that which can be safely delegated and that which cannot. The aim must be to delegate all duties which can be adequately performed by more junior staff who, by definition, are less expensive than the credit manager (see Figure 14.1).

Inquiries and information

The simplest job to delegate is the processing of paperwork and handling of inquiries, trade references in and out, listings and filing. Filing can, of course, be separated if this is a large feature within itself. This area might be called the 'credit inquiries desk'. The person in charge would act as a filter for the manager and save him having to break off from some urgent or important job just to answer a question which can be answered by the inquiries clerk. This clerk would also be responsible for keeping the credit bureaux registers up to date and processing special inquiries to the credit bureaux.

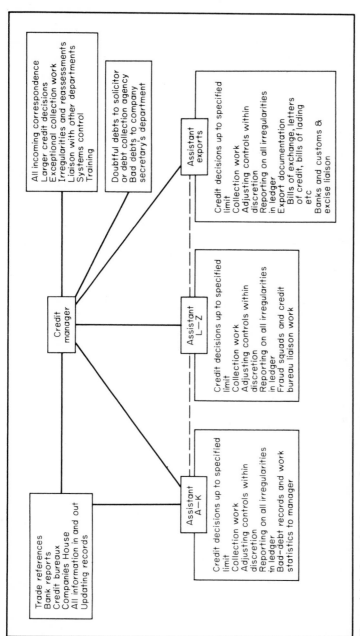

Figure 14:1 Organization chart for credit department

Bad debts

The next piece of delegation should relate to liquidations and legal
action. When a debt has passed a certain stage – that is, when there is
nothing more the credit manager can do about recovering it – it should,
as a bad debt, pass out of his hands either to a solicitor or to the
secretary's department, whose job it will be to follow up the liquidator
(or the solicitor) to obtain payment of dividends or other form of
partial recovery.

The credit manager may be likened to a doctor and the debtors to
his patients: when a patient dies the doctor ceases to be responsible; the
undertaker takes over. If the credit manager has to deal with debts after
the point when they should be considered bad, it will hamper his
attending to his first priority which is the prevention of debts going
bad.

Ancillary tasks

There are several ancillary functions which can appropriately be
undertaken as secondary functions by nominated assistants in the credit
department. For example, one may be responsible for keeping bad-debt
statistics and workflow charts. Another may make a speciality of
getting to know the people at the various credit inquiry bureaux and
maintaining good relations there as well as with members of the Fraud
Squad and even Customs and Excise. From time to time a credit
department will acquire information of a suspicious nature and the
opportunity to exchange notes over the telephone with these various
bodies will be mutually useful. In credit work it is often possible to
obtain revealing verbal information which could not be committed to
paper but this cannot be done unless contact has first been established
and then maintained.

Functions which can be partially delegated

Apart from the functions already mentioned, the main work of the
credit department will fall into two areas: (a) credit assessment, and
(b) collection work. Much of this work can be delegated to assistants
working under the credit manager's supervision.

Credit assessment

This aspect covers everthing connected with establishing credit for a new customer, making inquiries, fixing internal controls, informing other departments concerned, reviewing assessments, approving repeat orders and, in general, maintaining firm but flexible control. The inquiries clerk can be trained to obtain the outside information and may learn through this training how to evaluate it. From this experience will come the ability to judge whether it is necessary to seek yet further information or whether that already obtained is sufficient for the credit manager to make a sound credit judgment.

On the other hand, the credit judgment function cannot be delegated except to trained assistants who have gained practical experience through working closely with the credit manager who should encourage his trainees from the start to express credit opinions. He will have to be particularly careful in pointing out to them whenever they make a decision on insufficient information, which is a common error. People sometimes tend to panic when a request for credit is marked 'very urgent'. It is the manager's job to ensure that the necessary inquiries are still made, despite this pressure, and to encourage his assistants to make use of the telephone in genuinely urgent cases.

When, in the opinion of the credit manager, an assistant has reached the point where he can make a sound credit judgment, authority up to a certain amount – say £250 – should be delegated to him. This is quite a responsibility to someone who has never previously enjoyed it and the delegation of this type of authority should be done with the utmost care. At the same time the assistant should be given a block of accounts to look after in which there will be accounts in excess of his own delegated authority. It will be part of his job to report to the credit manager on all irregularities within that block, irrespective of whether the amounts outstanding are over or under his own authority. Thus this assistant will become the eyes and ears of the credit manager in this particular area, but the manager will still have to carry out periodic checks to see whether his delegation is working properly. These checks should consist of spot checks on certain key accounts and occasional inspections of the whole delegated area. This procedure will pave the way for further satisfactory delegation because, if the assistant's work passes both the spot checks and the overall inspection he may be eligible for further responsibility either by being given a wider area or by increasing his underwriting amount to, say, £500, or both.

Collection work

Much of this work lends itself to system and delegation. The pace of collection procedure will depend initially upon the company policy on granting credit and the terms accorded to each customer. If terms vary from one customer to another the records must show the terms for each customer so that any routine collection procedure swings into action neither too early nor too late but just at the right time. Knowledge of the terms of sale is vital to efficient collection work.

Much time is wasted by writing special letters to customers whose accounts are overdue. Because this operation is time-absorbing it is sometimes not completed. It is perhaps not so far from the truth to suggest that if your name begins with W you can, on average, obtain longer credit than your fellow debtor whose name begins with A. This is because most people looking after ledgers begin composing beautifully polite and lengthy letters to people at the beginning of the alphabet and then either run out of time or become bored somewhere between L and R. This is less likely to happen if a routine system is established and if correspondence confines itself to *A*ccuracy, *B*revity and *C*larity – the ABC of collection work.

The detail of collection procedure was dealt with in Chapter 7. Suffice to say here that the milder the tone of the letter the more the manager can afford to delegate; conversely he will want to be absolutely sure of his assistants before he permits them to send 'final applications' because one of these sent in error can cause serious repercussions. The manager should inspect the copies of all collection letters sent in his name; in this way he will be able to measure both the skill and output of his assistants and correct any tendencies to either slowness or impetuousness. From this it can be seen that much effective delegation can be made in comparative safety, provided it is controlled. Thus much of the routine which is the essential base of all good credit management can be handled by others under supervision.

Use of telephone

Another priority which the credit manager should lay down is which customers should be telephoned to urge them to pay their accounts.

Too much telephoning is expensive and is not necessarily effective, especially if the right person at the other end does not answer. Too little telephoning means that significant debts are outstanding longer than they need be and this costs the company overdraft interest. It also means there is less working capital in the business and it may mean forfeiting discount in the bought ledger department. The accountant should therefore be most interested in the credit manager's collection performance and he might do well to work out what size of overdue balance merits a telephone call.

In a situation where interest rates are 9 per cent a year, money costs ¾ per cent a month. An overdue debt of £2,000 costs £15 for every month it remains overdue. A debt of £4,000 costs £1 for every day it remains overdue. From this simple fact it becomes plain that, although telephone calls for debts of a few pounds are probably not worth while, the larger debts should be tackled by both letter and telephone. The credit manager must encourage the selective use of the telephone in all collection work.

Functions which cannot be delegated

There are certain functions which should on no account be delegated. These are, of course, the decisions involving a principle of establishing a precedent, or where an exception needs to be made in an exceptional circumstance, or where a change in procedure needs to be evolved.

Major credit decisions

The manager should not delegate the most important credit decisions because, even though his assistants may be able to make such judgments competently, he has to be the effective leader of his credit team and he must keep his hand in at credit assessment. Quite apart from this consideration, he is ultimately responsible for all departmental errors and he should in particular keep the direct responsibility for the most important credit decisions.

Selection of priorities

The two most important tasks facing a credit manager are the selection of priorities and the selection and training of his assistants. Priorities, in credit as in other areas, fall into two broad categories: (*a*) priorities in *time*, and (*b*) priorities in *importance*. When delegating, it is important to draw a clear distinction between the two: there is the task which may not be the most important task of the week but which must be done today; there is another type of task which is vitally important but which is not vitally urgent. When people have grasped the importance of doing things today and are able to allocate their priorities in correct order of time, they tend to think that they have achieved efficiency. However, it is only half the battle, because people can become so absorbed in the tasks of the day that there is a tendency to put off the less urgent but more important tasks altogether.

Establishing follow-up systems

The manager must institute a system of reporting or follow-up to ensure that both types of task are being tackled appropriately. A way in which to ensure that the important but non-urgent problem is tackled is to issue a written instruction on the subject, with a deadline date for reporting back. This last point is essential if 'drift' is to be avoided. A spare copy of this instruction should be filed in a date-file or 'jack-up' which it is the duty of the typist/secretary to pull daily. If the jack-up copy is dated two days before the deadline date and brought back to the manager at that time, he can inquire about progress on the task before it is too late. This encourages better staff relations than waiting the extra 48 hours to catch them out, as it were.

Some managers think it should not be necessary to give more than one instruction on a subject and, therefore, they should not have to remind their staff of tasks to be completed. This is all very well in theory and if it works it may be fine in practice too – but does it? The test of an efficient manager is whether his department works efficiently – not how it works – and if a timely reminder works better than none, no amount of theorizing will change this fact of life. It is probably fair to say that if staff never need to be reminded then they are not sufficiently busy.

It is quite insufficient to issue instructions and then leave the matter there. The manager must know for certian that the instructions are carried out properly and in time. If they are not he must find out why and rearrange staff and duties in such a way that his instructions are carried out properly and in time. He has not achieved efficient management until he has achieved this. The selection of priorities is, therefore, something which should not be delegated.

Assistants who have too much to do — perhaps temporarily — must be insructed to report the fact because there may be a choice of courses open to the manager. He can decide in which order the outstanding tasks should be tackled and he may be able to borrow someone else, less pressed, from another section.

Keeping flexible

A credit department must be adaptable. Crises may arise from time to time and special jobs may have to be undertaken at very short notice. It is vital to have a routine which establishes the norm but it is also vital to break from that routine in an emergency.

To give but one practical illustration: assume that a customer is in serious financial trouble and owes, say, £4,000. The credit manager should visit the customer without delay. He finds that the only worth-while asset in the customer's business consists of debts due by his customers. The credit manager reaches agreement to take assignments of the customer's debtor balances sufficient to meet his claim and he requires his assistants to help in carrying out this complex task. A large bad debt is thus avoided.

This type of exercise rarely has to be undertaken but when it does it has to be carried out quickly, efficiently and patiently. This illustrates the advisability of having a well-trained staff who can, in an emergency, leave their routine and deal with it. If a routine is established it is comparatively easy to return to it and pick up the threads again after the emergency has been dealt with.

Correspondence

One of the credit manager's keys to maintaining control of his department is to ensure that he sees all incoming correspondence, the tone of which will quickly show whether or not the department's extramural image is in good shape. Letters of complaint should always be answered promptly and, usually, these replies should be signed by the manager himself.

The credit manager should be a good correspondent and his letters should be an example to his staff. Unlike the sales force who make a personal impact upon customers, the credit department's image will depend almost entirely on its correspondence. It must, therefore, be as good as possible and the manager must read the copies of outgoing mail to see that the highest standards are maintained at all times. To sum up this question of correspondence, writing letters can to a large extent be delegated but reading them cannot.

Staff training

It will primarily be through this vetting of correspondence in both directions that the day-to-day staff training will come about. Quite apart from the problem of teaching staff to make the right decision there is also the art of putting it over in an acceptable manner. The right decision is only slightly more important than the right manner. The most brilliant credit brain will not reach a position of much responsibility if he cannot temper his knowledge with discretion and tact.

These are the points that the credit manager must watch at all times and, if he has delegated wisely, he will have time to watch them and time to see that the departmental organization is prospering.

Outside training should never be looked upon as a substitute for the daily practical guidance and experience to be gained in a well run credit department. However, there is much to be gained from joining the Institute of Credit Management which organizes both lectures and courses in addition to setting examinations.

Another useful course is Dun and Bradstreet's *Credit and Financial Analysis* which consists of sixteen chapters to read and fourteen study papers to answer. The papers are marked and constructively criticized by their examiners. This course involves a few hours' work each week for about five months and through this the aspiring credit manager can acquire much useful knowledge, some of which he would probably not acquire nearly so quickly just by working in a credit department.

Index

Accounts analysis forms and use 46-54
Administration of credit 3-4
 see also Managing the credit department, Organization of credit department
Administration of Justice Act 1970 118
Admission and offer to pay 115
Agency reports 9-10
Agents
 credit bureaux 9-10
 debt collecting 111-12
 del credere 150-1
 solicitors 112-13
Analysis of balance sheets 35-59
Assessment and control of credit accounts 72-84
 examples 74-82
 old and new accounts 73-82
 trade disputes 82-4
 see also Organization of credit department
Assessment for credit 52-4, 58-9, 193-4
 overseas 158
Assessment of company from balance sheet 54-9

Assessment of current financial situation 26-7, 54-5
Assets
 and liabilities 22
 balance sheet 23-9
 current 23-4
 fixed 23-4, 29
 valuation 41-2
Attachment of earnings 118
Attachment of Earnings Act 1971 118
Auditor
 certificate and balance sheet notes 33-4
 remuneration 21
 stocks and work in progress 26-7

Bad debts 120-33, 192
Balance sheet
 analysis 35-59
 assets 23-9
 liabilities 29-33
 specimen 24
Balance sheets
 and published information 13-15
 value of 22-3

Bank loans and overdrafts   31
Bank references   7-9
Bankruptcy   121-4
    debtors composition or deed
        of arrangement   123-4
    receiving order   122
Bankruptcy Act 1914   121
Bankruptcy (Amendment) Act
    1926   12ł
Bankruptcy proceedings and
    winding-up orders   119
Bankruptcy rules   121
Bills of exchange   63-4
    at term after sight   154-6
    payable at sight   153-4
Book value of assets   23
Break-up value   40-54, 58
    accounts and analysis form
        44-7
    calculation   42-3
    specimen   43
    valuation of assets and
        liabilities   41-2
Brokers and underwriters for
    insurance   137

Capital   32-3
Cash
    and credit basis   68
    balance sheet   25
    valuation of assets   41
Cash against documents   153-5
Cash flow   38-9, 52
Cash on advice of availability
    66
    on delivery   66
Charging order   119
Choice of computer   167-8
Collection agencies   111-12
    compared with solicitors
        113

Collection procedure routine
    88-92, 194
Companies Act 1948   19
Companies Act 1967   19, 20,
    38
Company accounts   19-34
    auditors certificate and notes
        33-4
    balance sheet   22-3
    balance sheet assets   23-9
    balance sheet liabilities
        29-33
    profit and loss account   20-2
    specimen balance sheet   24
Company accounts analysis
    46-54
    forms and their use   44,
        46-54, 56-7
Company assessment   54-9,
    193-4
Comprehensive Bill Guarantee
    scheme   149-50
Compulsory winding-up   126-7
Computer as management aid
    163-73
Computer control section
    164-7
Computer definition   163-4
Consolidated group accounts
    20
Contra
    accounts   69-70
    bills   70-1
Corporation tax   21
Cost of credit   5
Cost of insurance   144-6
County court action   115-16
    admission and offer to pay
        115
    judgment   116
    summons   115
Credit and Financial Analysis
    (Dun and Bradstreet)
        198

Credit bureaux reports   9-10
Credit information   5-18, 190
Credit insurance   134-46
   cost   144-6
   ECGD   140-2, 149-50
   factoring   142-4
   market   136-40
   risk   134-6
Credit registers   10
Creditors and accrued charges
   30-1
Creditors committees of
   inspection   127
Creditors voluntary winding-up
   125-6
Currency
   exchange risks   159-62
   transfer risks   158-9
Current taxation   31
Customer trading accounts
   assessment   73-82
   credit limits   185-7

Debenture interest   21
Debentures and registered
   charges   14
Debt collecting
   credit department   194
   other agents   111-13
Debt collection letters   92-109,
   197-8
Debt collection policy   87
Debt collection procedure
   85-109, 194, 197-8
   exceptions   92-6
   letters   96-109, 197-8
   routine   88-92, 194
   terms and discounts   86-7
Debtors   25, 41
   composition   123-4
   death or disappearance   120-1
   deed of arrangement   123-4
Deferred liabilities   29

Definition of credit   1
Del credere
   agents   150-1
   risk   135
Delegation in credit department
   190-8
   complete   190-2
   partial   192-5
   undelegated functions   195-8
Demand draft   157
Depreciation   21, 29
Direct information   15-18
Directors loans   31-2
Dividends   21
   proposed   31
Doubtful debts   92

Elements of credit   1-4
Endorsement of bills and
   guarantees   64-5
Enforcement of judgment
   117-19
Enforcement of payment by
   solicitors   113-14
Equity   20
Establishment of policy
   for collection   87
   for credit   175-6
Execution against goods order
   117-18
Export collection procedures
   156-7
Export credit assessment   158
Export Credits Guarantee
   Department   140-2,
   149-50
Export trade development
   147-51
   ECGD   140-2, 149-50
   factoring   150-1
   merchants and confirming
      banks   150
   the banks   148-9

Extended credit
  debt collection   92-3
  terms of sale   62-3

Factoring   142-4, 150-1
Fifty per cent cash/credit   68
Final letter   91
Financial management ratios
  25, 27, 30, 36-7, 46-53,
  54-9
Fixed assets   23-4, 29
  fixtures and fittings   42
  freeholds and leaseholds   42
  investments and loans   41
  machinery and vehicles   42
Follow-up systems   91-2
  establishment of   196-7
  see also Routine for debt
  collection
Formation expenses in balance
  sheet   28
Fraudulent preference   121,
  122, 127-8

Garnishee order   118-19
Goodwill as an asset   28
Guarantees
  endorsement of   64-9
  for loans   31
  from parent company   14

High balances debt collection
  93-4
High Court action   116-17
  appearance   116
  enforcement   117-19
  judgment in default   116
  summary judgment   116-17
  writ   116

Information for credit purposes
  5-18
Inquiries and information   190
Institute of Credit Management
  198
Insurance market   137-40
  brokers and underwriters
  137
  credit insurance companies
  138-40
  operation of credit insurance
  137-8
Insurance market intelligence
  136
Insurance through factoring
  142-4
Internal communication network
  177-88
  liaison with despatch   183-8
  liaison with sales   181-3
  lines of communication
  178-81
Investments and loans   28, 41
Irrecovable letter of credit
  151-2

Judgment   116
  enforcement of   117-19
  in default   116
  summary   116-17

Large customer debt collection
  94-5
Legal action   77, 115-19
  county court   115-16
  High Court   116-17
Legal proceedings   110-19
  agents and solicitors   111-13
  court action   115-17
  enforcement of judgment
  117-19

Letter of credit   151-2
Letters and reminders   88-91,
    99-109
Liabilities
    balance sheet   29-33
    valuation of   42
Liquidation of limited companies
    124-7
    compulsory   126-7
    creditors committee of
        inspection   127
    creditors voluntary winding-
        up   125-6
    members voluntary winding-
        up   124
Load over load terms   67-8
Long firm   12-13

Machinery valuation   42
Managing the credit department
    195-8
    correspondence   197-8
    follow-up systems   196-7
    major decisions   195
    priorities   195-6
Members voluntary winding-up
    124
Merchants and confirming banks
    150
Mid-month reminder   88-90
Moratoriums   130-2
Motor vehicle valuation   42

Nature of credit   1-4
Net worth of company   39-40,
    55-8
Non-paying customer collection
    95-6

Official Receiver in Bankruptcy
    122, 126, 127

Open credit   67
Open-item system   170-3
Organization chart for credit
    department   191
Organization of credit
    department   168-70
    189-98
    and the computer   168-70
    junior management tasks
        192-5
    management functions
        195-8
    routine tasks   190-2
    training   198
Overseas terms of sale   151-6
    bill of exchange at term after
        sight   154-6
    bill of exchange at sight
        153-4
    irrevocable letter of credit
        151-2

Paid-up capital   14-15
Patents and trade marks   29
Payment grading chart   184
Policy
    for collection   87
    for credit   175-6
Post-dated cheques   65-6
Pre-set credit limits   68-9
Procedure for debt collection
    85-109
Producing collection letters
    92-109, 197-8
    exceptional   92-6
    routine   98-9
    specimens   99-109
Pro-forma invoicing   66
Profit and loss account   20-2
Profits
    assessment   55
    level of   38-9

Promissory notes   65
Proposed dividends   21, 31
Provision for bad debts   132-3
Purpose of credit   3

Receivers   128-30
see also Official Receiver
Refer-all transaction lists   187-8
References   6-10
   bank   7-9
   credit-bureaux   9-10
   credit registers   10
   trade   6-7
Reports
   credit-bureaux   9-10
   representatives   15-18
Representative reports   15-18
   specimen   16
Reserves   21, 32-3
Resources needed for credit
   1-3
Responsibility for credit
   management   176-7
Restarting stopped credit   185
Risk
   currency exchange   159-62
   currency transfer   158-9
   del credere   135
   factor in insurance   134-6
Routine for collection   88-92,
   194
   see also Debt collection
   procedure

Sales staff and credit limits
   185-7
Sales-ledger information   10-13
Services provided by factors
   142-4
Share capital and reserves   32-3

Shipment and contracts insurance
   policies   140-2
Short credit terms   66-9
Short-term transactions
   collection   93
Solicitors and debt collection
   112-13
Staff training for credit
   department   198
Statements of account   88, 90
Stock
   as balance sheet asset   25-8
   valuation   41
Stocks and work in progress
   23, 25-8, 49, 51, 53
Stopping deliveries   184-5
Summary judgment   116-17
Summons   115

Taxation   21
   current   31
Terms and discounts   86-7
Terms of sale   60-71
   additional safeguards   63-6
   contra accounts and bills
      69-71
   extended credit   62-3
   for export   151-6
   monthly credit   61-2
   short credit   66-9
Trade disputes   82-4
Training of staff   198

Undue or fraudulent preference
   121, 122, 127-8
Use of computer   163-4
Use of credit   1
Use of solicitors for collection
   112-14

Use of telephone in collection
    work   194-5

Valuation
    assets   24, 41-2
    liabilities   24, 42

Winding-up
    compulsory   126-7
    creditors voluntary   125-6
    members voluntary   124
    orders   119
Working to a pre-set credit limit
    68-9
Writ of *fieri-facias*   117